SOUL
MATES

Also by Jenny Smedley:

SOUL MATES

Magical and mysterious ways to find true love

JENNY SMEDLEY

piatkus

PIATKUS

First published in Great Britain in 2013 by Piatkus
This paperback edition published in 2014

A CIP catalogue record for this book
is available from the British Library.

ISBN 978-0-7499-5840-4

Typeset in Palatino by M Rules
Printed and bound in Great Britain by
Clays Ltd, St Ives plc

Papers used by Piatkus are from well-managed forests
and other responsible sources.

 MIX
Paper from
responsible sources
FSC
www.fsc.org   FSC® C104740

Piatkus
An imprint of
Little, Brown Book Group
100 Victoria Embankment
London EC4Y 0DY

An Hachette UK Company
www.hachette.co.uk

www.piatkus.co.uk

Whatever our souls are made of, his and mine are the same.

Emily Brontë

Contents

Acknowledgements

I dedicate this book to my husband, Tony, who has been and always will be my friend and soul mate, my confidante and sounding board, my lover and companion, as well as the only judge I'll ever need, and the father of my son.

I want to thank Piatkus and my agent, Sallyanne Sweeney, for showing faith in this book.

I'd also like to thank Anne Newman for her diligence and patience doing my copy-editing.

And Zoe Goodkin, my editor at Piatkus, who has done a wonderful job of helping me make this book as good as it can possibly be.

Acknowledgements

Introduction

In my capacity as an international columnist and adviser I am asked many questions, most commonly things like:

- Who is my soul mate?
- Where is my soul mate?
- Why hasn't my soul mate found me?
- Will I ever meet my soul mate?
- How can I find my soul mate?
- How can I tell if I've already met my soul mate?
- Did I know my soul mate in a past life?
- Why did the person I thought was my soul mate leave me?
- What do I do if my soul mate dies or chooses to leave me?
- Do I have more than one soul mate?

The questions above are universal – I don't know anyone, famous or otherwise, who hasn't asked one of them at some point in their life.

In this book I'll unravel the mysteries behind that most sought-after state – the state of being in love with the right person and making it last. I'll be examining the various types of soul mate you might encounter in your life, and help you learn to differentiate between them, so that you can recognise them for what they are. I'll also explore the magical and mystical means that can help nature along.

Let me first of all say that my beliefs surrounding the subject of soul mates are very much based on the premise that we have all lived before. This, I'm convinced, is fundamental to a belief in soul mates – because unless we've known each other before, how can we possibly expect to recognise each other when we meet again in this life? It's the 'knowing' that sets soul mates apart from others in our lives, and that knowing comes from having shared certain other-life experiences.

So what's the secret to achieving a successful soul-mate relationship? Many hypotheses have been offered: compromise is a common one, and this does have some bearing on achieving a balanced relationship, but it isn't the whole secret. Fidelity – this too plays a large role, but if your union is right there won't be any question of being unfaithful; you'd never risk hurting someone you truly loved by being unfaithful – not in exchange for a few minutes of passion and certainly not for the length of a full-blown affair. Children – it's true that children can bring a couple closer, but it's also true that they can pull them apart too; couples do still sometimes stay together 'for the sake of the children', but when they do it's obvious their union wasn't a true one.

The truth is that there is just one secret to a long and happy relationship and it's very simple: *you have to commit to the right person.*

As obvious as this might sound, I know from personal experience how easy it can be to marry the wrong person, while thinking they're the right one. Our social upbringing is based around being a success, and that success is generally perceived to include a husband or wife and children. No wonder then that some people rush into the first thing that seems right – especially given that women have the additional constant reminder that their biological clock is ticking. I used to think that things would change, but although the emphasis might have shifted away from marriage, a solid relationship is still what most parents wish for their offspring, and 'How's your love life?' seems to be the question most frequently on their lips. Because of this pressure, it's not surprising that many gay people marry in their haste to prove themselves 'normal', whatever normal is, and live a lie for many years until their true nature is forced 'out of the closet', often ruining lives in the process. Divorce also ruins lives. Husbands are often left having to buy out a wife, leaving themselves penniless, and wives are often left caring for children and trying to explain to them why 'Daddy' has gone.

So it all sounds pretty grim, doesn't it? But if you're having trouble trying to find a soul mate of any kind, there's clearly something else you need to accomplish first. You need to concentrate not so much on being 'successful' in the eyes of others, and not to rely on others to make you happy and keep you cheerful, but on being happy within yourself. If you can become independently happy, then everything else will fall into place – including the possibility of finding soul mates (and yes, I intended that plural) who need not necessarily be partners. In this way, your energy and the way others perceive you will be very different from the way it was previously, and others, including your soul mates, will be more attracted to you and find you more easily. By filling your life with soul mates, you'll lead a rich and fulfilled life automatically, enhancing your happiness, and you'll do and be who you're meant to be.

You might ask why you should take any notice of what I have to say on the subject of love and soul mates. Well, I'm someone who did get it right, which I think you'll agree is quite something in this day and age, although I only found my soul mate after going though many twists and turns.

My husband Tony and I have been blissfully married for forty-two years. I used to think that we were the norm – that everyone who 'fell in love' was happy for ever. But over the years, all around us, friends and relatives have split up and divorced, and our relationship now stands out as very unusual. You need only switch on the TV today to see how everything from commercials to soap operas portrays the relationship between husband and wife as competitive at best and combative at worst. The more you see of partners making snide comments, trying to win an argument or score points against each other, the clearer it becomes that soul mates are not that easy to find, and that so many people are still searching for theirs. Some of them have obviously settled for second best because they're afraid of ending up alone, and have found themselves in the middle of a constant stream of skirmishes, instead of the fairytale state of har-monious support and love they'd dreamed of. But, I'm here as living proof that the fairytale is still possible.

Tony and I first met when I was ten and he was twelve. The funny thing is that although I'm sure the seeds were sown at that time, neither of us really remembers much about it now. We were both in hospital. He was having his tonsils out and I was having my adenoids out; so there we were, two kids under stress, shar-ing the unpleasantness of surgery and a first stay in hospital.

We didn't meet again until I was seventeen and he was nine-teen. It's very odd to think that for all the intervening years we'd been revolving around each other in very similar orbits, but never quite connecting. I feel that this was all to do with us even-tually meeting at the right time in our lives. At the time, I'd just come out of what I'd thought was a serious and very real part-nering. I'd been hurt and badly let down by a boy called David and, at first, I thought my heart would break. It wasn't until much later in my life that I realised sometimes we get 'dumped' for our own good. After all, if we hadn't broken up, I might not have met Tony. I'll explain more about why that happens later in the book.

When Tony and I met for the second time a few weeks later, it hit me like a bolt of lightning. We were at a dance, and we were with different groups of friends. I was being heavily pursued by a young lad called Rob, but I only had eyes for the tall, slim, brown-eyed stranger, whom I caught watching me surrepti-tiously every now and then. I got rid of Rob as soon as I politely could, but by then Tony had left, giving friends a lift as he was one of the few among us who drove.

Later, a friend called Pam confided in me that she was going to make a play for Tony, and having little self-confidence I pretty much gave up, thinking I could never challenge her. But to my surprise, Tony rejected Pam in much the same way as I had Rob, and asked me out instead. We soon became inseparable, and we were married in 1969 – the year of the first moon landing – when I was nineteen and he was twenty-one. Since then we've had a son, lived in nine different homes and, all in all, had a very inter-esting life together.

However, fifteen years ago I found myself in real trouble – the sort of trouble only a real soul mate could help me with. The emo-tional experiences I went through, always with Tony by my side, showed me without doubt that he *is* my soul mate, meant to be with me for ever. They also taught me the true value of having one. Without him, I would undoubtedly have gone down the very rocky road of depression, which might possibly have ended in my demise. In the end, all was well, but only a true soul mate could have coped with the situation and survived it. I will also explain more about that in future chapters.

For now, suffice it to say that having experienced love both good and bad, real and counterfeit, and survived a rollercoaster journey with my relationship not only intact, but even stronger than before, I feel qualified to help other people find real and sustainable love – to know it when they see it, and to find it when they don't.

I think Tony's and my story demonstrates the importance of finding your real soul mate, rather than heading down paths that end up in heartbreak. I could easily have agreed to marry David, if he'd asked me, because – like so many teenagers – I was 'in love with being in love', but that path would almost certainly have ended in divorce and I might, at best, have seriously delayed being with my true mate or, at worst, never managed to unite with him at all.

In the pages that follow I will help you to avoid potential pitfalls. I will:

- Show you how to recognise what is real and what isn't, by defining the different types of soul mate you might come across
- Demonstrate how to understand why they are in your life
- Help to mend your heart if you've already had it broken, offering sound advice on how to recover and get going on your journey to real love.

I've included many true stories of others' experiences too. These come from people who have written to me for advice, from friends and acquaintances and also from people I've discovered during my research into this subject.

So if you feel alone and are starting to think that your whole life journey is one you must travel in isolation, just open your heart, mind and soul to the words in the following chapters. Trust that the universe knows what's in your best interests, that everyone can find other travellers to walk alongside them and that this, most certainly, includes you.

CHAPTER 1

What Is a Soul Mate?

The subject of soul mates is much more complex that many people think. When asked what a soul mate is, most will come back with the wrong answer. They think it is always equivalent to a husband, wife or lover. They automatically think of a soul mate in terms of a partner, chemistry, a lifelong union, and so they are often disappointed, because this is not always the case. People also tend to believe that there's only one type of soul mate they can have as a partner, and that if they don't find that one unique person they will never be happy. This is incorrect too. It's possible to have many different soul mates of different kinds and to have a very happy and fulfilling life with any one of them.

In this chapter I'm going to take away some of the mystery surrounding soul mates, and explore the different kinds you might encounter. I believe there are four main types of soul mate (more of which below), and each can play a different role in your life, helping you to become a complete and balanced person with joy in your heart.

What is a soul mate?

A soul mate is literally and simply a friend to your soul, and can take many forms, some of which might surprise you. Soul mates can be the opposite sex to you or the same. They can be related to you, or just be your best friend. They can be your lifelong partner or they can come into your life fleetingly, perhaps to teach you something and then leave. Soul mates are connected to you on a soul level, and that connection can never be broken, not by being apart, nor even by death. This association can and does travel through lifetime after lifetime.

By now you're probably realising that to know a soul mate is very fortunate indeed. If you already know you have one or more in your life, treasure them. If you don't have one, then don't give up, because almost everyone finds a soul mate of some kind.

What kinds of soul mate are there?

There are varying opinions as to how many kinds of soul mate there are, but my experience has led me to believe in four main ones: Eternal Flame, Twin, Teacher and Comforter.

A soul mate of any of these four types is someone you feel very close to, and with whom you feel very much in tune. It's someone you know you can rely on to love you, no matter what. This person knows you very well and you know them in the same way, even if you only just met. You feel at one with them, there are no awkward silences, no contrived small talk, and their companionship is comfortable and relaxing. You know you can always call on this person and they will take care of you emotionally and make time for you. They make you feel valued, and yet they don't flatter because they will always tell you the truth, even if you don't want to hear it, but they would never deliberately hurt you for kicks. There are no insecurities, because you know you can trust them completely. They will never judge you, and will have no choice but to love you. And while they would make an admirable and reliable sexual partner, it doesn't have to be that way.

ETERNAL FLAMES

This is what most people envisage when they think of the perfect fairytale soul mate. This is someone who feels like half of you. Whenever they're absent your life almost seems to go 'on hold'. They know what you're thinking and they offer you total, unconditional love. In other words, whatever you do and whatever you become, they will never stop loving you. This can be the perfect relationship, and it's what I have with my husband. This soul mate is the stuff dreams are made of. There will be no battlefields – maybe minor skirmishes as both parties have to learn lessons – and this partnership truly embodies the cliché that the two people together are greater than the sum of their parts. There will be no unfaithfulness because the love they feel goes right down to soul level, and it will be impossible for them to hurt each other – indeed, they will never desire another anyway. There will be no jealousy between them either, because to hurt an Eternal Flame soul mate is like hurting oneself, and each one feels the pain and the joy of the other.

However, not everyone will find this kind of soul mate in every life they live because the strong dependency that can be formed isn't always a good thing and might not be right at this particular stage of their existence. Because of this we may live some lifetimes apart from our Eternal Flame, just to make sure that we learn to rely on ourselves and not on someone else. This is a tough concept and one I will expand upon later (see Chapter Three). But there are alternatives and one can have a happy and fulfilled life without meeting one's Eternal Flame in this life.

I use the word 'Eternal', because while other soul mates can change their interaction with us, the Eternal Flame is constant. If they are in our lives, there will be no mistakes. The union is certain and cannot be resisted. Whatever the circumstances, you will simply have to be together.

Sometimes those people who pursue us hotly, may be assumed to be our Eternal Flame soul mate, whereas another who takes a more measured and assured approach with no 'fireworks' at all will end up being the 'one'. So how can you tell the difference? It's in the way you feel: do you feel uncomfortable with or even threatened by a person's ardent advances or does it make you feel happy, even if you're not inclined to respond? If you're not comfortable with the person, there's a danger of being swept off your feet and into a relationship that will drown you spiritually in the end. You'll be comfortable with a soul mate – that's the overriding factor. It's a good thing to feel wild, sexual abandon as well, of course, but it will still be a feeling that you're comfortable with. If you feel a tiny vestige of fear of them, or want to have space between you to 'recover' from their presence, they are not your soul mate. So rather than looking for a flash of lightning when you meet someone, as well as attraction you should also look out for a feeling of coming home.

I have chosen to put Zoe's story here because she describes so beautifully the way an Eternal Flame makes you feel. She also describes other types of soul mate she's encountered and so demonstrates that there isn't just one – or even just one type.

Zoe's story

I knew Aaron was my soul mate when I met him, even though we were both in other relationships at the time. There was that instant connection that was deeper than lust when we looked at each other, and there was recognition at soul level – that sense of 'I know this person'. We kept everything above board by ending our other relationships, but it felt easy and natural and meant to be; easy because we both did exactly what we said we would all the time – no lies, no games – and always felt there was a deep understanding between us from the beginning. The relationship has been through really tough times, but the deep connection has always remained. We're better people for being with each other.

Soul mates are mutual. If your partner doesn't love you the way you love them, they're not your Eternal Flame. I think true soul mates both recognise the connection. I've met other kinds of soul mate along the way, although none with the extent of love I share with my husband. That deep part of me has always understood the lesson from the 'meant-to-be' meeting of this person who changes your life (and this can include friends, not just lovers). The relationships have a deep level of just 'knowing', and even when the intensity of the relationship disappears, the connection is still there.

Jacky's story of Eternal Flames meeting has an equally happy outcome of an entirely different kind:

♡♡ Jacky's story

One day, when I was in my teens, I was in our local pub with my boyfriend. A crowd of guys walked in, some of whom I recognised from school, and they seemed to be celebrating. They were county hockey players and had just won their game. The group got rowdy, but I was enjoying the fun and attention (my boyfriend was not). Suddenly, one of the guys in the group dared his hockey-player friend to sit on my lap. I vaguely recognised him. He lived quite close to me and I'd seen him arrive home from work in a pinstripe suit. He worked in a bank and drove a nice car – very different from my motorbike-riding boyfriend. He also had a lot of red hair. Not my usual type at all.

As this guy walked over, I began to giggle – my boyfriend was not amused! I moved so he could sit on my lap and, as he did so, a voice spoke in my head: 'That's the man you're going to marry.' It was completely clear in my mind, as though I was being 'reminded' of a cosmic plan. Having carried out his dare, he jumped up and walked away, leaving me staring after him, bemused, thinking: what just happened?

The evening went on and I managed to chat to some of the hockey players. It was my eighteenth birthday that weekend and I was having a party, 'Why don't you all come?' I urged them. They seemed interested, especially my red-haired friend, but then I felt embarrassed and muttered, 'But it's mainly family and might be rubbish . . .'

The night of the party arrived and I made an extra-special effort to look good. The redhead didn't turn up and I was bitterly disappointed. I remember my boyfriend and I had a big row. At one point he tried to push me down the stairs, but luckily my mum appeared just at that moment and my boyfriend went home. I knew it was time to get rid of him!

For the next year I would see the redhead around from time to time. How can I arrange to meet him again? I wondered. I used to borrow my nan's dog and walk endlessly backwards and forwards, past his house, but our paths never crossed.

Time moved on and most of the guys had gone on to university. But now it was holiday time and many of them were home. Would they be going to the local pub again? With an excuse in mind, in case anyone wanted to know what I was doing there alone, I walked into the local pub – and I was in luck. My hockey-playing friends were in there and pleased to have some female company, and one of the group immediately bought me a drink, followed by another. Two hours passed quickly and the young men were ready to leave. My red-haired friend was one of the designated drivers, so hadn't been drinking. He asked if I'd like a lift home and I said I would, although I could easily have walked as it was only ten minutes away.

He opened the front passenger door for me – a good sign – and we dropped the others home, one by one. Then it was just the two of us in the car. Would he ask me out now? Surely he was interested. Five minutes passed, then ten, then fifteen. Unable to bear the disappointment, I said goodbye and walked into the house. Was that it? Perhaps I had been mistaken about the voice a year earlier?

The next day I was determined to try again. It was the last day before the guys returned to university. I managed to get the redhead's number and found an excuse to ring him. We chatted for a few minutes and I clumsily told him I was bored at home. He took the bait! 'Would you like to go for a drink? I'm bored too!' He picked me up an hour later. It was the longest wait of my life. (I'd got ready before I'd made the call, just in case!)

It turned out that when he'd dropped me off and I'd been hoping he'd ask me out, he'd been waiting for me to invite him in for coffee! That night I did invite him in and one of my kind sisters made him a drink. I was far too shy!

So the voice was right all those years ago, after all. John – my red-haired friend – and I have been together for thirty years and married for twenty-eight of them. We have two daughters and a wonderful granddaughter.

It didn't happen easily – I had a year's runaround – but he was the one. It had been planned before we were born. The reality is that I probably didn't need to do anything at all. I believe that if I'd waited, the plan would have unfolded naturally. He was already mine – my soul mate. Oh, and the funniest thing of all? He no longer works for a bank; and he too now rides a motorbike!

When you meet an Eternal Flame soul mate, there is no doubt, and the need to be with that person is irresistible. They may not fit the picture you had in your mind, or appear on the surface to be a perfect match – they might be older, not of the gender you'd anticipated or of another culture – but all these potential obstacles will be surmountable because their soul will be a perfect match for yours. It is their soul that you will recognise on a deep level.

Any kind of superficial love you may have experienced in the past will be totally eclipsed. And, as Zoe said, it is always mutual. People who are asked what true love with an Eternal Flame feels like often say something like, 'True love is difficult to explain to someone who has never felt it, but you will know it when you feel it.'

TWIN SOUL MATES

In a way, Twin soul mates are one step down from Eternal Flames, but they can sometimes be the most confusing type of all because while love is certainly and obviously there between you, you have to discover whether your relationship is one that will last and help you achieve what you need to in life.

Part of the confusion with Twin souls comes from the fact that the two of you will be very alike in many ways. Twin souls are exactly that, a mirror image of each other, and you are certainly very closely connected to one another on a soul level. Because of this you can indeed 'complete' each other and, as with Eternal Flames, the two halves together can be stronger than the sum of their parts. However, the opposite can also happen. For instance, because you will both have similar personality traits, this can, at times, make you argumentative. Or you might both want to be dominant or submissive, and so not give each other what you need. You might both want to be the strong one or both need support. However, your Twin soul will share the same values as you and often want to strive for the same things, which will make you a formidable team. You will often have the same taste in food, music and literature, even support the same sports teams, so you will see eye to eye on a lot of things.

A Twin soul will seem familiar to you right from the first

meeting, and indeed they *are* familiar, because you will have known them before, in other lifetimes. They'll make you feel comfortable because in a past life they were probably your friend or partner, and it's tempting to think you can just take up where you left off with each other. It's an instinctual pull, and sometimes it is right. But this is where the trouble can come because often you're together just to help each other out, and you're not meant to be lifelong partners. Not realising this, and perhaps also being under pressure from social peers to commit, you might marry and then further down the line find the need to part. Or you may be meant to be partners for a short time, perhaps to create specific children, and once that has been done your need to be together fades.

If your Twin soul mate leaves, you can be left feeling devastated by what seems like total betrayal. However, your Twin can sometimes make a wonderful lifelong partner, especially if your respective Eternal Flames aren't going to be with you in your current lives.

So a Twin soul mate can be one of many things and their purpose can change throughout their lives. They can be a lifelong supportive partner or just be there for a short time after which their role might change to that of a Teacher or Comforter (see below). Accepting these changes, if they happen, can be the key to your future happiness.

Edwina is a friend of mine from the USA. Here is her story:

Edwina's story

I met up with my soul mate in this life in April of 1993. We were on some of the same committees in our town and had meetings together quite often. I remember having a discussion about him with a friend before we had technically met because he kind of made me nervous. She said that he was mean and that I should stay away from him. I figured that this would explain the feelings I got every time I was around him. It was almost like I was scared of him.

One evening, we found ourselves outside after a meeting and we started talking. The minute he looked into my eyes and I into his, I knew something was very different. It felt like looking into my own soul. It was a very comfortable, familiar feeling. We talked for a couple of hours that evening and I felt like we had known each other for ever. The fear went away. I was enchanted. I realised later that it was not really fear I had been feeling, but that it was my spirit reacting to his presence. I had never had any thoughts about soul mates before, and I truly don't remember where the idea first came from, but I knew very early on that we were connected in a very deep way.

I found myself seeking him out and wanting to be around him as much as possible. This was pretty easy at that point because we typically would have up to five meetings a week together. I knew that he was drawn to me as well. I could tell by the way he was with me.

The part that was a little confusing was that at the time, I was married. He still is, though I have since divorced. At first, both of us misunderstood what was happening and took it as a physical attraction. We discussed it many times, and I have to be honest, it *was* partly a physical attraction, but we also knew that it was something much deeper than that.

We did not take the physical part any further, but we did start to spend a great deal of time together. We would go out after meetings and just sit and talk. He told me that he had never been so comfortable with anyone, and I knew that I was at home when I was with him.

Then, strange things started to happen. We found that we were having the same dreams at the same time on the same night and, after this had happened a few times, we started paying closer attention. We could recite the dream to each other and finish each other's sentences about what happened next.

A couple of times, we would find that we would have the same injuries. Once, I hurt my finger on something, and he showed up the next time we saw each other with an identical injury on the same finger. He couldn't remember how it had got there, but it was the same size and shape as mine.

There were many times when I would somehow just know where he was. One time, we had just left a meeting and I was driving home when I suddenly knew that he was at a local drive-in restaurant and that he wanted me to join him there. It was not near his home, or a place he usually went to, but I listened to my spirit, and I went, and there he was. I got out of my car and into his truck, and his first words were, 'What took you so long?' This happened to us over and over.

He would often know if I was upset about something and he would call to make sure I was all right, or he would 'test' us by going somewhere and telling me spiritually to come and I would.

Finally, in late 1994, everything came to a head. His wife did not like us spending so much time together and his daughter wasn't fond of it either. Things got so uncomfortable for him at home that he told me we needed to back away from each other. I understood, but I felt like my insides were being ripped out. I knew that we would never be alone spiritually. I told him that, and he agreed. Still, it was a very difficult time.

After that, we both sort of changed paths and started doing different things. He stopped going to the meetings we'd attended together and eventually, so did I. However not a day went by that I didn't think of him.

Once, a couple of years later, we happened to see each other in town. I stopped and we talked for a while. I had changed jobs since we had last talked, and I was trying to tell him where I was working. He said that he always knew where I was. I believe that is true. We are still so connected spiritually. I know that he is my true other half, although we will probably never be together in this lifetime.

Two years ago, he started coming back to see me. That lasted a while and then he stopped again. I don't know for sure why he does that. It makes me ache every time. There have been times when it hurt so much that I wondered if there was a way to ask the universe to undo it. However, to do that would be to have a part of myself die. He is as much a part of me as my arms or legs.

Today, we still email each other sometimes and I send him birthday and Christmas cards each year. I haven't seen him in a long while now, but I feel his presence just as strongly as the first day we met.

I have never loved, nor will I ever love anyone else the way I love him in this life. It is not the same as a physical or sexual relationship; it is not even the same as being married.

I truly believe that our spirits are one with each other. When we finally reach the end of our paths in this world and are returned to the sprit realm, I believe that we will be joined together and that we will fill the void that has been left in each of us. What a joyful day that will be.

Edwina's story demonstrates how confusing it can be when you encounter a Twin soul mate, which is what I believe happened in this case. Her Eternal Flame may still be destined to come into her life, although I'm sure that until he actually does, she won't be able to believe it.

TEACHER SOUL MATES

There is a saying, 'When the pupil is ready, the teacher will appear'. Teacher soul mates will sometimes come into your life, usually temporarily, to enable you to learn something vital to your soul's progress. They won't normally be a partner (although this can happen) and the relationship can be challenging and difficult and the lesson can be harsh. Once the lesson has been given, the Teacher will sometimes vanish as mysteriously as they appeared, and this can cause upset and confusion to you, unless you understand their purpose in coming into your life for just a short time.

Sandy's story

My son came into my life in the role of teacher. I didn't understand what was going on for years. After he reached adulthood, he would keep falling into debt. I'd bail him out – he'd get into debt again. It was like money just slid through his fingers. His dad was long gone and I didn't know what to do for the best or which way to turn. I was behind with the mortgage and nothing I said seemed to get through to my son.

Eventually, I was advised to have past-life regression to see if something in the past could account for our troubles. Much to my astonishment my son agreed to go with me. It was incredible because he hadn't done anything I'd asked for years.

Together, in a joint regression, we discovered that in a past life I'd been his wife. I'd been a waster. I'd spent all our money on clothes and jewellery and made us bankrupt. It was a life I'd denied because I'd never wanted to face it, but once we'd both recalled the same salient points, I knew it had to be true. My son was my Teacher soul mate because he taught me that love is more important than possessions. This lesson – and understanding it – made me stop trying to control him and his money, which I admit I had been guilty of. I let him live his own life and wasn't too surprised when, within a year, he'd straightened himself out and made good. He also paid me back what he owed me. It seems that once I'd learned the lesson I was free to love my son unconditionally.

Difficult lessons indeed, but Sandy's story shows you that there is a way through such difficulties. Once Sandy understood what the lessons were, the mere fact of her acceptance of them was enough, and I'm sure her relationship with her son improved immensely afterwards.

COMFORTER SOUL MATES

These people can step into your life sometimes just to say a specific thing, to bring comfort and companionship when you're feeling alone or when you need some advice to help you make a tricky decision. They can often become lifelong friends once they do appear. They think the same way as you and are always there for you, but you never see them as potential partners. They're often the opposite sex, and yet there is no sexual chemistry between you. This is a true, platonic relationship, and this kind of soul mate isn't even always human, but more about that later. This type of soul mate can also come along to bring you solace and companionship if, for some reason, you aren't going to be with your Eternal Flame in this lifetime. In Carmen's case I am sure that was why she had her mother as a soul mate.

♡♡ Carmen's story

I believe that we have Twin soul mates who aren't necessarily partners. I, as a whole person, have two halves. My one Twin soul mate was my mother. In every picture you see of us we are touching, cuddling, holding hands. When I was with her I felt whole – to the extent that when I got married I felt as though something had been taken from me, as though part of me was missing. It was as if when I was with her I could breathe.

Every night when I came home from school or later work, there would be a huge meal cooking and freshly baked cakes, and on weekends there was always a big dessert and a full cooked breakfast on Sundays. When I stood by her watching her cook, it was like we were parts of a jigsaw; we locked in.

My mother encouraged me to read – by the age of eleven I'd read *Jane Eyre*, *Little Women*, *The Black Arrow* and so many more – and as a kid on a winter's night, I would snuggle by her feet in front of a roaring fire with a book or I would do a little embroidery. Mum would be knitting or just resting. I realise now that what I was feeling was greater than time, something eternal.

When my mother died it was like half of me died too. It was like I couldn't breathe properly any more. I would keep turning round to look for something, then realise it was her. I feel as though I have just half a body and keep expecting people to ask where the other half is. I know that I will not feel whole until we meet again.

My Eternal Flame soul mate and I are not meant to be together this lifetime. I did glimpse him once, but that's another story. My mother and I will be together again though I am sure – and for eternity.

I think Carmen is right. She and her Eternal Flame aren't meant to be together this time, so she had her mother – who some might actually see as her Comforter soul mate – to help her through a difficult life without him.

In the belief that they have only one soul mate, people often put themselves under enormous pressure to find that unique 'one', even though it would be impossible for everyone to achieve this. But as I have said, you don't necessarily have just one soul mate – or even just one of each kind. You can have several. So while it might go against everything you thought and believed, the knowledge that you have more than one soul mate should make you feel a little more optimistic about meeting one. The only kind that you seem to have just one of is the Eternal Flame. That has been my experience, and it's what I've come to feel sure of.

Take the short quiz overleaf to identify the kinds of soul mate you have in your life already. If you don't think you've found any soul mates yet, it might help you to recognise when you do.

Identifying your soul mate

1. When you first met your soul mate, did you instinctively feel that you already knew them?

2. When you talk, does the conversation almost always stray into deeper subjects, revealing a lot about both of you?

3. Was the closeness between you apparent very quickly, even if you didn't go straight into a romantic relationship?

4. After a while, did the exact circumstances of how you met become a little blurred, as if it might have happened several times in different ways?

5. When you met, did you feel as if you had been somehow saved by this person?

6. If you ever have an argument, does it hurt until you make up, and then does the anger dissipate very quickly?

7. Did you develop subtle little signs or code words, so that one of you always knows when the other wants to leave a dinner party or social event without having to actually say so?

▶

8. Do you often know what your partner's thinking, even when you're not together?

9. If you're apart and you close your eyes, can you sometimes visualise where the other person might be?

10. Do you sometimes know when your partner has a problem, even if they try to hide it – and vice versa?

If all of your answers were 'Yes', that means you have found your Twin or Eternal Flame soul mate. If some of your answers were 'No', it doesn't mean you haven't found a soul mate, just that they're more likely to be of the Teacher or Comforter kind. If all your answers were 'No', the person you're thinking of is not a soul mate and you should be wary of placing too much trust in them.

Have I got a soul mate?

People who seem to be unable to meet a suitable partner often start to wonder if they even have any soul mates. I can assure you that everyone has some kind of soul mate in every life, whether it be Eternal Flame, Twin, Teacher or Comforter. However, when people ask 'Do I have a soul mate?' they are usually referring to their Eternal Flame.

Everyone has an Eternal Flame soul mate but, as mentioned earlier, there are lifetimes in which we must learn to exist without our Eternal Flame in order to make sure that we don't form too strong a dependency on our other half. In these lifetimes, our

Eternal Flames will remain in our lives in spirit and, in rare cases, will reach out to us as a spirit guide. The idea that your Eternal Flame soul mate may not exist in human form in every lifetime can be a hard concept to accept. However, you can be reassured by the fact that your Eternal Flame is with you on a spirit level throughout every lifetime and that you can connect with a different type of soul mate in order to fill this void.

How important is it to find a soul mate?

It is true that you can be happy, and should be able to create happiness without soul mates, but finding them does hold the key to the ultimate realms of fulfilment. Let me show you what I mean by looking at the celebrity culture.

Celebrities in today's world are always partying, always with friends and always having a good time. They have it all: they have all the money and fame they could ever have aspired to and they're an elite bunch who have every chance of happiness. Or so it seems. We see their glamorous lifestyle as the epitome of contentment. But is it? The majority of celebrities have one big failing: they seem to be incapable of sustaining a good relationship – and if you take a really close look, you'll find that underneath the glitz most of them are unhappy most of the time. Failed marriages are what normally come with fame. Cut off from normal life and normal people, they tend only to meet other needy celebrities. And anyone else? Well, they simply don't trust them: is the person attracted to them or their fame? How are they to know? Consequently, their 'field of choice' is limited to other celebrities and finding a soul mate becomes very difficult for them, and so they rarely do.

If you could take celebrities out of the limelight for a moment and ask them what would fill them with ecstasy, most would say a soul mate, and most would agree that they'd swap all of the adoration and money, for that one thing.

So remember, money alone can't make you happy. Clothes, cars, rubbing shoulders with the famous, being chased by paparazzi and having people screaming your name – none of this can make you totally happy for ever. If you are already happy within your own skin, then these things may well make you feel somewhat more secure or temporarily joyful. But a partner who understands you and is always on your side – who is a 'friend to your soul' – is the real answer, and any celebrity will tell you that. If you find one who is truly content in their own skin and doesn't just find happiness when living out a fantasy role on stage or in front of the cameras, I can guarantee that you will also find they have a real soul mate in their life – whether in the marital sense or in some other mentoring role.

Soul mates can help each other in many ways. It's not just about being partners to share life, or being someone who can be trusted, a person to love and be loved by or a loyal confidante. There's more to it than that. I believe that as well as a life journey, we're all on a soul journey, and we can rely on all the kinds of soul mates outlined above to come and help us progress with this. Soul mates always tell us the truth, so having one – or many – helps us to grow, to push us back on to our rightful path if we stumble, to understand life's lessons and to develop intellectually. A soul mate enables us to release emotions and show and embrace love without fear. They support us in times of need without judging, forgive our mistakes, lead us to a better place and allow us to lead them when the circumstances are right, to give us freedom when we need it and to pick us up when we fall.

All of these things can come from a lover, a friend, a parent, a brother or a sister. Soul mates are many and various and have numerous roles to play. And never forget that somewhere out there your soul mates are waiting and hoping and praying to find you too.

CHAPTER 2

Are Soul Mates Always Human?

In this chapter I'm going to explore the question of whether animals can be soul mates – a subject that some might find controversial. Much of the controversy is removed, however, if you accept what I've already said – that soul mates are not by any means always partners.

Many people have told me stories of a pet that they feel an incredible bond with – something so deep they feel it has to be on a soul level, and I've had experience of this myself too. I was given the phrase 'a spark of your soul' by a psychic, and this describes the role of soul-mate pets very well, as I believe they are literally the containers of a tiny spark of our own souls, and that this is why we feel so devastated when they pass, for we are actually losing a part of ourselves. For many people, pets are often their main – sometimes only – comforter and company, and their innate ability to love unconditionally is a lesson to us all. So as soul mates pets can often play both the Teacher and Comforter roles.

Some people might not be able to accept this concept, but I'd ask them to stop and reconsider what I said earlier: a soul mate is, literally and simply, a friend to your soul. Many millions of people throughout the world have been failed by society in general: they've been failed by the system, failed by their friends, failed by the state, failed by their families. But some of them have been saved from a life of loneliness and depression by a pet. A pet dog, cat or even a goldfish can fill a room that would otherwise be sterile, lifeless and unwelcoming with 'company'. They give the person a sense of 'being important' to another soul. They can listen to the outpourings of a lonely heart without judgment or pity. They are intensely loyal, perhaps showing the person the only unconditional love they've ever felt. Who are we to say that these pets are not soul mates of the comforting kind?

If you believe, as I do, that animals have souls, then they have also had past lives. If you can accept that they've had past lives, then you have to accept that they've known people during those lives, and that some of them come back to bring comfort to people who would otherwise be alone. Furthermore, animals are sometimes teachers too, because when you think about it, in a lot of ways animals are more spiritual than people. They are certainly more intuitive, more instinctual, more energy-based and a great deal less Machiavellian than most people. Certainly, some animals prey on others, but unlike man they only kill to live, or to learn how to live. They bear no malice towards the animals they kill and eat, nor do they kill for reasons of wealth, prejudice, hatred or power. Animals are honest, they treat everyone the same and they are capable of giving love without making demands.

Just as an aside, past-life regression can be especially helpful with relationships with pet soul mates. What may have been seen as behavioural issues in a pet can turn out to be the animal flagging up some past-life issues you need to resolve. Some pet communicators like Madeleine Walker, actually regress pet and owner together, with some astonishing results. (See also p. 197.)

Here are some stories of animal soul mates that people have sent to me.

♡♡ Consuelo's story

My terrier mix Abby showed me she was my soul mate throughout her life, but it wasn't until a week after we lost her that I realised how strong that bond was. As an artist who specialises in animals, I'd tried many times throughout Abby's life to paint a portrait of her. I could paint everyone else's dogs, but never my own. Many times while I was working in my studio with Abby at my feet, I would talk to her, saying that I wished I had more freedom in my work and didn't have to be the type of artist who had to paint every piece of fur and make my work totally realistic.

About a week after her passing I had an extremely strong urge to sit down and try to do a portrait again. As I started working, I felt a wonderful sense of freedom and started using every bright colour available. Within two hours I'd completed a beautiful portrait of Abby in a style that was completely different from anything I'd done before! I then went on to create a whole portfolio of dog portraits, all of them in this new-found style, and everyone who saw them loved them.

I always knew Abby was my soul mate, but never expected her to be my muse after her death. These portraits are proof to me that she is still with me and will always be there for me. It's so comforting to know that I never really lost my best friend and that, in one way or another, she'll always be at my side.

If you feel that your pet is a soul mate, then why not visit an animal communicator or pet psychic because if your pet can tell that person something personal they have observed about you, you'll never need to doubt your beliefs again. Mike's story is a good example.

Mike's story

Oliver came into our lives unexpectedly following the very emotional loss of our elderly cat Mollie. A few weeks after losing Mollie my wife answered the door to a lady who was holding a kitten and said that if we did not take him, he would have to go to a cats' home. My wife was thrilled to have him and named him Oliver. Their bond was apparent from the word go, and after we obtained a very small harness and a lead for him, the pair of them would go for walks around the village – Oliver trotting alongside my wife, his tail in the air. Six years on, they still go for weekend walks, although nowadays there's no need for the harness or lead!

My wife talks to Oliver endlessly and is convinced that he understands a great deal of her conversation, staring into her eyes and at times cocking his head to one side, as if genuinely paying close attention. When she read an article in a Sunday magazine about an animal psychic called Jackie Weaver, who'd communicated with William Roache's (from *Coronation Street*) dogs, she immediately wanted an appointment with her.

An email was sent and a date was set, but then my wife became nervous, concerned that she would not know what information to ask Jackie to seek. However, Oliver led the conversation and made her smile when he even commented about her endless dusting, as she is so very house proud! Oliver actually brought this up because having watched my wife – now in her more senior years – as she climbed steps to dust, he was apparently afraid that she would fall and hurt herself. He said that he would prefer her to climb up on to things when I am there, in case anything should happen.

Oliver's adoration of my wife shone through; he even commented on how much he loves listening to music with her, sweetly pointing out that she snores gently when she dozes off with him on her lap. The relationship between them is so special and, as he explained to Jackie, he knew that he had come into our lives at a time when love and comfort were needed. He has most certainly brought that and so much more. If, like my wife, you want to share in your pet's inner thoughts, I highly recommend a 'cat chat' for a most unusual, interesting and thought-provoking experience.

I have, in fact, myself been featured by Jackie in her book about talking to celebrities' pets (see Recommended Reading, p. 197). She had a long conversation with my dog KC, and although they'd never met before she correctly identified an old shoulder injury, our dog's favourite walk, and some design work KC had watched me doing on the computer a few days before.

Animals like those described in these stories are different from other pets. I've owned many dogs and horses over my life, but most of them, while infinitely loveable, can't hold a candle to one particular dog. Her name was Ace and we adopted her from a welfare centre.

We already had two dogs, both rescues, and when we started thinking of getting another one we weren't expecting anything beyond the normal dog–owner relationship we had with the other two. The rescue centre only had one dog. She was thirteen weeks old and the woman told us on the phone that she'd been abused and was scarred. She asked us not to take the dog unless we were sure we wanted her, because she'd already been homed twice and returned as 'unstable' and 'insane'.

We met up at a quiet industrial estate, halfway between our homes, and a white van pulled up next to our car. The woman from the centre got out and a young dog on a lead followed her quietly. The dog sat beside the woman in a most unpuppy-like way – more like an old dog. She was black, except for pink, wrinkly patches of skin on her chest. We were told that she'd been scalded – almost to death – and would never grow hair on those patches. I crouched down, and the puppy got up and crossed over to me. She sat down beside me and leaned against my leg. In that moment something happened. A link was formed that would never be broken. It was like she'd been waiting for me.

The woman was pretty surprised at this turn of events, but after making sure we were committed to the dog, she got back in her van and drove off. This was the start of a totally incredible fifteen-year journey.

Ace was unlike any dog I had ever owned. She was part of me. I know that sounds cliché, but it is true nevertheless. She grew into a big, fierce-looking German Shepherd cross Labrador, but she never lost her scars. During her time with us she saved some of our lambs that had been rejected by their mothers, cleaning them off with her own tongue when they were cold and wet. She saved my life from a rogue ram that knocked me down and would have fatally head butted me if she hadn't intervened. She was the most fabulous dog and I pitied those prospective owners who had rejected her because they missed out on the dog–owner relationship of a lifetime.

Ace was a very healthy, happy dog until she was twelve and then she had a mammary tumour. The thought of losing her nearly drove me mad, but after surgery she pulled through, although she lost a nipple in the process. When the time finally came for her to leave me, I honestly thought I would die from the pain. I had her put to sleep in our home, and I held her and reassured her while she passed. Sitting in the room with her body lifeless in front of me, I wanted to go with her. I had never experienced a loss like it in my life. I determined that I would never have another dog, for how could I ever go through this pain again? Besides, I didn't want any other dog – if it wasn't her, it would always be second best.

Six months later my husband and I were on holiday in Sedona in Arizona, and I went for a psychic reading. The psychic told me that she had a message from a big, black dog with a grey face. It was Ace. She wanted me to know that she was a 'spark of my soul' and that we would, therefore, never be really parted. She also said that today she was 'young again'. It was 13 September 2004.

When we got home I pondered on what she could have meant by these statements. On the table I found an advert from a local newspaper advertising a litter of black puppies. Something made me call the number and I was told that they had been born on 13 September. Coincidence? Possibly, I thought, but

I had to check it out. We went to see the puppies and that's when déjà vu kicked in. While most of the litter poured out into the garden, one puppy just sat like an old dog and gazed at me. I crouched down and the puppy walked across and climbed into my arms. I looked down at her face. Could it be? Was it possible that Ace had come back?

The puppy grinned, seemingly at my thoughts, and she rolled over, showing me her little fat, pink tummy. I looked down and a smile filled my face with joy as I saw that the puppy had been born with one nipple missing – the same one Ace had lost in surgery.

There was no room for doubt. But the final proof came – if it were needed – a couple of months later when another psychic, an artist, contacted me. She said that a black German Shepherd cross Labrador had been in touch and sent through a drawing she wanted me to have, with the message, 'This is what I look like now'. The drawing was totally identical to a photograph I'd just taken of our new/old dog. It was the same dog, there was no question.

Over the next few years, KC, as we called her, grew little circles of white hair in exactly the same places as where Ace had been scarred. And I came to believe wholeheartedly that special soul-mate animals like this truly are a spark of our souls, which is why it hurts so much when they taken from us by death. Today though, I am comforted to know that they do sometimes come back to us, and even if they don't – like all true soul mates – they will never be parted from us for ever.

Just like humans, animal soul mates are persistent when it comes to finding and being with you, then staying with you in spirit form, even after they've passed away. The next two stories demonstrate this beautifully:

Hazel's story

I think my Maltese dog Millie was my soul mate. About three years ago, I walked into a new-age shop that was newly opened, and waited for my appointment for a reading. One of the women at the counter asked me if I had a little white dog (I had gone alone to the shop). I replied, 'Yes – but she passed away two years ago.' The woman then told me she could see her by my side. I'm really pleased she still walks with me.

Jacqueline's story

My sister sent me an email with a picture of Che Guevara, a pointer dog, who was skin and bone, telling me, 'This is your new dog!' I'd already decided that I wouldn't have another dog for at least a year after my previous dog had died three months earlier. He was a darling Dalmatian called Dillon. But hey ho, I went to meet Che Guevara.

When I was there, another little dog called Pepa was asking me to take her too, and I can remember saying, 'I'm sorry, I can only afford to have one dog,' and left it at that. When Che was delivered to my door, the woman had another four dogs in the van, so I said she should let them out in the garden so they could stretch their legs. I was looking at Che and he was so nervous that I thought: my goodness, this dog needs a buddy! At that moment Pepa jumped into my lap, almost as if she was saying, 'Me, me, me!' She's been glued to my side ever since.

I feel sure that Pepa was sent to me, and have sometimes thought that she is one of my previous dogs in a new life. It really does feel that she's my soul mate, as she's very sweet and loyal (and cheeky). That's how I ended up with two dogs – Che Guevara and Pepa – just three months after losing my Dillon. So much for the dog-free year!

Jacqueline's is by no means the first story I've been sent like this. Dogs and other pets will sometimes worm their way back into our lives irresistibly. I have heard of the same thing happening with everything from horses to guinea pigs.

This next story shows how a pet can come into people's lives to make a very meaningful contribution, rather than just being a faithful companion. I have many stories about pets that have saved lives and protected people, but this one has a very strong element of synchronicity in the perfect timing needed from the dog, which could be a Twin or Teacher soul mate to either Margarita or her father.

♡♡ Margarita's story

I dreamed before we bought Buffy that an angel was going to find us the most beautiful dog he could, and that she would be very special. Well that's all very true as I knew when I first saw her big blue eyes that Buffy was my new puppy. (I had lost my beloved Yorkshire terrier a few years before when he died peacefully at the grand age of twenty.)

A few weeks ago, I woke up in the middle of the night to hear Buffy barking, but I could tell instantly by the pitch of her bark that something was very wrong. She tends to stay awake in the night and check on my father, who hasn't been well for a few years now. Then I heard my dad shouting out for my mum and the words, 'I'm covered in blood!' I rushed out to see my father lying on the floor in a pool of blood.

I ran to call an ambulance while my mum tried to help my dad. He told her he'd passed out on the landing. Apparently he'd fallen, hit his head and had been unconscious until he woke to find Buffy licking his face and barking simultaneously!

As I rang for the ambulance my dad was saying his goodbyes to us, obviously believing he was going to die. Buffy sat with me while I waited for the paramedics at the door. It turned out that when Buffy had tried to wake my dad by licking him, his pacemaker had 'jumped' inside his heart and started working. This had saved his life. The blood was from his nose when he had fallen and hit his head. I have no doubt Buffy really was sent to us by an angel.

Margarita's story shows that certain animals will come into our lives to perform an act that can change everything for us. This is exactly the sort of thing a human soul mate will do.

We have a tendency to think of some animals as being natural enemies, such as cats and dogs, monkeys and tigers, birds and cats, etc. But animals, in their spiritual and non-judgmental way, are quite capable of turning such preconceptions on their head and making the most unusual of alliances. I believe this is because at certain times, their almost angelic ability to see each other as pure energy, totally overrides what might be their natural prey and predator roles. I've seen film footage showing how one animal can sometimes see right past the physical body and into the soul of another which convention would label as their foe. They can create soul pairings with their own kind, as well as with others, sometimes most unexpectedly, to form genuine soul-mate relationships.

Although I've concentrated here on stories about dogs and cats, pet soul mates can come in all shapes and sizes, from a mouse to an elephant. For those who look for 'good-news' stories instead of doom and gloom, the media is full of accounts of amazing friendships between animals of the same species, and even stranger ones between animals of different species. There are many accounts of dogs and cats that have stayed beside a stricken or even dead companion for many days, and have to be persuaded to leave them, even if they are in a dangerous situation. There are stories of deep friendships between dogs and cats and dolphins and internet footage showing dogs that regularly swim out to play with dolphins in the water and cats interacting with dolphins from the edge of a boat. There are stories of dogs and elephants, hippos and tortoises and almost every combination you can think of. But perhaps most convincing for me is the footage and photographs I've seen of husky dogs playing with polar bears, which are considered one of the most dangerous and ferocious animals on the planet. Animals certainly are some of the greatest Teacher soul mates that exist. (See Resources, p. 194 for web links showing how animals really can teach us humans a lesson in how to get along peaceably with each other.)

CHAPTER 3

I Already Know You

Do you believe in past lives? To me it seems obvious that they must exist as our lives are much too complex to be sorted out in a single time span of eighty years or so. We interact with so many people, so many questions are left unanswered, so many experiences not experienced and so many dreams remain unfulfilled – including, for some, finding an Eternal Flame soul mate – that there has to be more than one piece, or lifetime, in the puzzle, if it's all to be resolved. However I haven't always felt this way.

I was brought up as a Catholic, and Catholicism does not believe in past lives. I lapsed when I was about nineteen because I felt the church was too much like a very rich, big business, but it wasn't until I was forty-five and had my own experience (see pp. 48–156) that I came to understand that past lives were real. Only once it had been forcibly proven to me did I really start to think about the concept fully. In this chapter I'll be showing you how and why you should perhaps believe in past lives too.

Why do we have multiple lives?

The conventional answer to this is so that our souls may learn and grow through experience, and that is something I believe in too. I go further though. In my book *Soul Angels* I put forward a vision I had been shown by my angels, which showed me that earthly souls are actually angel-based. That is, I believe that in order for angels to evolve they had to experience being human, that a new breed of angels was created specifically for this purpose and that a spark from each angel was then placed into a human body. This spark is what we call our soul. As each body dies, that spark or soul passes to a new body that goes on to take it through new experiences. Once we've achieved enough and our soul sparks have progressed enough to trigger evolution in our angel, they'll go back to the source – the angel root – permanently, and we will once more become evolved angels ourselves. Our soul mates will make this leap too, and from then on we'll be together with them for ever in angelic form.

If my theories and beliefs about past lives are new to you, and you've never before thought about having known a soul mate in other lives, or even about having had past lives at all, you might be asking why you have to have multiple lives, or what happens after you or your soul mate dies, or whether you have to come back over and over eternally. You might worry that having found your soul mate, you might have to come back without them or that if you die after them and go to spirit, they may have already gone back to earth in a new body and so you'll miss them. Let me answer these questions for you.

Any soul that ever existed leaves the greatest part of themselves in the world of spirit at all times. It is only a small part – a mere spark – that descends to the earth plane to enter a physical body and experience life as a human being. The other part, the angelic part, stays in 'heaven', or whatever you like to call it. This means that someone to whom you are eternally joined at soul level will be there waiting for you, even if their spark is still on earth. And the same applies to you – the greater part of you remains in the spirit world at all times. So whoever dies first, they will not be alone in the spirit world, but will be with that part of their loved one that has always stayed in spirit. And the one who's left behind to 'finish their business' will one day join them too.

Once people accept the concept of past lives, they often then want to know if they've met their partner before in another time and place. There is a very good chance of this, whichever kind of soul mate we're talking about. After all, we're talking about a soul connection, so it seems obvious to me that something must have gone on between you before this lifetime. How else would such a deep connection have been made?

There are many different categories of past-life soul mates and so many different scenarios can be very confusing. I'll go into more detail about them in the next chapter. For now, however, I'd just like to look at the power of a past-life connection between soul mates, as demonstrated by Nancy's story.

Nancy's story

Several years ago I wrote a memoir with an attached workbook and have been facilitating workshops for women with it ever since. One particular aspect of my life experience always intrigues the women who work with me. Initially, when I was writing the book, I was surprised to find myself writing about a boy I'd only known for three weeks. Back then, I was doing research for a book on alternative education, visiting free schools all over the country. When I walked into the building that housed the Santa Barbara Community School in California, I noticed a boy with a huge afro standing on the stairs and wondered: who is that? But I told myself I was being a dirty old woman (I was a mere twenty-seven) and went on with my job as a journalist. However, once the boy and I started talking, we couldn't stop. I did my job, but I also spent hours with him.

He touched me spiritually in a way I had never been touched before, and seemed more in tune with my feelings, thoughts and deepest self than any man I had known – all of which I disregarded. I was already living with the man who would become my first husband. I'd completed graduate school. I lived in New York City. The boy was working as a janitor. He was about to begin city college, but had no idea what he wanted to do. I believed the gap between us was too great, left Santa Barbara and left him behind as well.

I had no idea what happened to him, but when I visited my daughters in Los Angeles years later, I knew I needed to find him. I didn't think we'd become involved; I just wanted to find out where his life had led him. Although his name was not in the Santa Barbara telephone directory, his brother's was. Within hours of my initial query call, he called me back. His name had changed from Lorenzo to Wonono, which was surprising. When he suggested driving down to LA to see me the following day, I was more than willing. I expected the afro when I opened the door, but found a balding older guy standing on the stoop. Once we both got over the initial shock of how each of us looked thirty-plus years later, our experience of each other was the same as it had been; we could not stop talking, and did so for almost nine hours.

Within months we were visiting each other on a regular basis, though neither of us knew where we were headed. At the end of that year, he moved up to Washington, where I now live. During those months we learned that what we had experienced all those years ago had been real. It has been a struggle for us – two people from such different backgrounds – to form a relationship, but our souls had known each other instantly, and they still do, and this has made the struggle worthwhile. We've been together for almost seven years now, and we both know this is for life. In the years between us finding each other again he'd married and divorced, and I'd had several relationships, but none of them had worked out. I do believe that having a soul mate is essential for me in any long-term committed relationship. The depth of our connection is often astonishing. As for the name change, that is a whole other story.

There's no doubt in my mind that these two had been together in previous lives. This is because of the age gap that at first seemed insurmountable, but in the end proved unimportant given the scale of their love. When two souls have been Eternal Flames, nothing else matters – not age, gender, colour, race, class or religion. Nothing else matters at all.

Barbara's story shows how a soul group (a group of souls who have been together in other lives, and often come back together for an agreed purpose – see also pp. 56–60) can be formed with friends and family members:

♡♡ Barbara's story

I have three children. One daughter – Rose – calmly told me at the age of two all about when she'd been my older sister. But what was amazing was that my sister, on her deathbed, had asked me to have a child so that she could come back and be my baby girl. My daughter and her twin brother were born one year and five days later.

My best friend died twelve years before my other daughter – Cathlene – was born. During her illness, she'd told me of her desire to come back as my child and even wanted to discuss her future name. 'No,' she said, 'Not Mariah! I'm already Mariah. I want a new name.' I was an unmarried college student at the time and didn't think too much of it, but after Cathlene's birth, my friend's sister contacted me. She'd been to see a psychic who had told her that her sister had been born as my daughter. She'd known nothing of her sister's request, nor did she know that I had had a new baby.

I'm astounded that two women have asked to be my future daughters. It's a flattering and a wonderful gift.

My own story shows how complex a meeting with past-life souls can be:

♡♡ My story

The nightmares I was having were graphic, extraordinarily real and very frightening. They always ended up with me screaming out the name Ryan. Those nightmares were only one part of the depression I was experiencing some years ago now.

I was married to Tony and I loved him dearly, but even our blissful marriage couldn't take away my strange despair. As my depression deepened, the irrational feeling of loss grew, the nightmares became more frequent and the questions became more intense. Who was Ryan? Why did I dream about him constantly? Why was I dreaming about another man when I had my Eternal Flame right beside me? And in my nightmares, Ryan and I were always dressed in clothes from a past time – why was that?

Then one day, as I wandered aimlessly through a shopping centre, shrouded in a haze of bizarre sadness, feeling totally cut off from those around me, I passed a butcher's shop. As the meat cleaver fell into a side of beef, I fell unwittingly into the past.

The scene in front of me changed, and a broadsword wielded by a kilted warrior was plunged into the body of a dark-haired man. It was shocking in its bloodiness. I knew that the man who had been slain in front of me was Ryan. When I 'came back' I was hopelessly disorientated and felt I was losing my mind.

During the following few months whenever I was alone in the house, I lived in fear of myself and of what I might do. One afternoon though, things changed dramatically. I felt different, as if some revelation was to come. I heard, whether in my head or outside, I don't know, the words, 'Turn the TV on'. I had no choice but to obey this strange order. Inexplicably, as if to make absolutely sure I didn't miss the image, the same picture flickered over and over again on the screen, and for a moment everything stopped for me. The TV showed the face of Garth Brooks, a country singer I'd never heard of. He was a stranger and yet, in a second, the pall of sadness that had overshadowed my life since the age of fourteen evaporated.

Tony and I found that romance blossomed once more in our relationship. Although the changes in me seemed to be enough, we had yet to find the link between modern-day country singer, Garth Brooks and the mysterious Ryan of my nightmares. Then, one night, the euphoria we'd been enjoying was savagely shattered as I experienced another nightmare and witnessed Ryan's death in full.

In the background was a small castle. (I found out later that it was Lumley Castle on 29 August 1640. Although the dates and places didn't seem to match at first, because the main battle with Scotland took place outside Newcastle on 28 August 1640, I discovered that the Scottish army would have passed through Lumley Castle on their march to Durham, which they took on 30 August. Records show that the castle was indeed involved in a minor skirmish and sustained some damage.)

Ryan stood frozen to the spot, armed only with a shield. Soldiers in kilts were running from the cover of a stand of trees, screaming battle cries, crazed with bloodlust. Ryan was struck across one arm and then run through as I'd seen before. He fell to the ground and, in his dying moments, he reached out, seemingly trying to grasp an unseen hand. He stretched out desperately, his blood-soaked fingers striving to touch someone. As he reached out he said one final word – 'Madeleine!'

Ryan from the nightmares bore an uncanny resemblance to Garth Brooks from the present, but this dream threw up a new mystery – who was Madeleine?

It wasn't until someone suggested that these dreams and

visions might be past-life memories, and that I might be Madeleine, that I gave reincarnation (the repeated rebirthing of a soul that has lived before into a new body) any consideration. I started to think I might try regression under hypnosis, and before long it had become something I *had* to do.

As I sank into that first hypnotic trance I was transported back to the seventeenth century and finally started to discover who Ryan was. As well as the information I gleaned from regression sessions, I also met other members of my soul group from that life (a group of souls who have been together in other lives and come back together for an agreed purpose), and they helped fill in the gaps. I found these people in various ways: some had read my book and it had resonated with them so strongly that they were compelled to get in touch with me; some were involved in media coverage of the story and, while sceptical at first, they soon came round – first to understanding and accepting it, then realising that they too had spontane-ous memories of that life; some came forward to help with publication and only understood later that they were motivated by the fact that they were part of my soul group and had been in that life too. One woman in particular had actually been experiencing visions and her family thought she was having a nervous breakdown, but in fact, it transpired that she had been Ryan's mother in that lifetime.

I discovered that Ryan was born in Ireland in the early 1600s. Caitlin, his mother, died from overwork when Ryan was just twelve years old. Although he did his best to support his two sisters, inevitably, because of the times they lived in and the poverty they endured, they succumbed to malnutrition and disease. Ryan fled to England to try and make a new life.

Several years later, after finding work where he could on farms and smallholdings, Ryan ended up in Hambledon near the home of the de Port family. (The name de Port came from someone else's regression, but it sounded right to me as the family had French Catholic connections. I never recalled the name myself as I think my unconscious did not want to accept that I had ever been a part of that family.) As Ryan neared the estate, he came across Madeleine de Port just as two ruffians were assaulting her.

I remembered being Madeleine, the aristocratic daughter of Edwin and Rebecca. Rebecca died when Madeleine was six years old, and her father remarried four years later. Madeleine never got along with her father's new wife Margaret, always believing that she had married him solely for his money and position. Eventually, an uneasy truce was established between them, but this was shattered for ever when Ryan Fitzgerald appeared on the scene.

The day they met, Madeleine had been out riding her horse alone. She fell off and was knocked unconscious, whereupon the two ruffians had tried to molest her. Ryan came along in the nick of time and saved her. Madeleine took her hero home and was dismayed when her parents treated him like a criminal. But her defence of him was total and unshakeable. Margaret and Edwin saw the danger signs and tried to keep the two of them apart, but it was too late. Madeleine had found her love and would never let him go.

When Ryan finally admitted his love for her and asked her to marry him, Madeleine accepted readily. They got married in secret and returned together to face her father's and Margaret's fury. Nancy, the cook, was the only friend to Ryan in the de Port household, and she was the only supporter of the young couple's love, even though she knew the master and mistress of the house would never accept it. I recalled many episodes of the three years that Ryan and Madeleine spent together on my journey of rediscovery.

Margaret and Edwin resorted to all manner of trickery and treachery in an attempt to destroy the love Ryan and Madeleine felt for each other, but it became clear that the young couple could not be parted, except by death. So eventually, Margaret brought death to Ryan. The couple were forcibly torn from one another's arms as, in desperation, they clung fiercely to each other's hands, but their fingers were prised apart and Ryan was taken prisoner by men the couple were led to believe had come from the King.

In reality, Edwin had used his political clout and wealth to have Ryan conscripted into the English army by men in his pay, and sent into battle against the Scots, where he was killed. I had witnessed his death many times in my nightmares and visions.

It became clear to me that just as Madeline had been reincarnated as me in this lifetime, Ryan had been reincarnated as Garth Brooks, and it was also clear why rediscovering him restored to life on the TV screen, had relieved my depression. But one other question remained. What happened to Madeleine after she lost the love of her life?

Almost as soon as I'd asked my subconscious this question, which was about two months after my first vision of Ryan's death, the nightmares returned – only this time I

saw Madeleine's descent into despair. Locked in a room for
two days and two nights following Ryan's disappearance,
going insane with terror at what might be happening to him,
Madeleine's fate was sealed. Once she was released, she
roamed the woodland where she and Ryan used to walk and
lay down in the bluebells where they used to lie together.
She could not live without him and, believing she could see
his ghost, she followed him back to the house, up the stairs
and into the attic. Looking down on to the courtyard below
and thinking she could see Ryan with his arms outstretched,
she jumped to her death.

After this nightmare, Madeleine wouldn't let me escape
from the emotions it had stirred up. I awoke many times
with the cry 'Ryan!' echoing through my soul. I now shared
Madeleine's quest and I realised that to close the circle for
her I needed to reunite her with Ryan. The only way I could
do this was to take her to him in his current incarnation –
I had to take her to Garth Brooks. This was very difficult
though as he's incredibly famous. To complicate matters
further, however, Garth is based in the USA and rarely travels
to Europe, and I've always been afraid of flying, so the idea
of me going to America seemed to be out of the question.
In any case, he was too well protected by his management
team for any requests to meet him to reach him, so my quest
was looking more and more impossible. But I knew that
Madeleine would never let me go until I laid the ghosts of
her own personal history to rest.

In the meantime, Tony and I searched for and found
evidence of my past life. We revisited the church where Ryan
and Madeleine were married and the house where they
had lived.

I also managed to see Garth at a rare concert in Ireland, and although I was far away from the stage, an amazing thing happened. From the age of fourteen I had suffered an undiagnosed abdominal pain which disappeared quite suddenly right after the concert. The pain had been in the same place as where Ryan had been run through, but I also found out that Garth Brooks has a scar in the exact same place on his body, apparently the result of a car crash in which his body was skewered by a piece of metal. That made perfect sense to me, having heard that we sometimes inadvertently 'recreate' scars from past lives on our bodies.

This episode made me even more certain of my quest and with Tony's support and with Madeleine pushing me on, I overcame my lifelong phobia of air travel. I boarded three planes in one day with Madeleine giving me the courage I lacked alone, and went to the USA. I met Garth Brooks' manager and attorney and was able to convince them of my sincerity, but meeting the man himself still seemed impossible as he was out of town.

I had almost given up all hope when I got a psychic connection with him and although everyone thought he was in LA, I knew that he was there, in Nashville, and I was able to find him so that a meeting could take place after all.

As Garth approached me, I saw his clothes transform into those he had worn as Ryan in the 1600s. As we moved closer together and our hands just naturally reached out to each other, I could see Ryan and Madeleine's hands being pulled apart. As our hands touched, Garth became Ryan on the battlefield, his bloody hand reaching out to find Madeleine's. Their hands met. The circle was closed.

My story of Twin souls meeting had a happy ending because it was much easier for me than for some others. I had no doubt that I was already with my Eternal Flame – Tony – and so I knew I wasn't meant to be with Garth Brooks and there was no misunderstanding on my part. Ryan was a Twin soul mate, a one-time partner, and it had been right at that time. I believe I'd felt drawn to see him again because I (or that part of me that is still Madeleine) needed to close the circle on that life and the terribly traumatic manner of their parting in order for my soul to be healed. This healing then change my life beyond recognition. It's interesting that Tony does not appear to have been in that lifetime with us, although he has been in most others, so it was obviously a life I needed to live without depending on him.

However, if I hadn't already been with my Eternal Flame in this life, you can see how I might have mistaken the situation between Garth and me for something other than what it was, and possibly ended up heartbroken through unrequited love. Sadly, some people find this does happen.

In this life my past-life memories changed me dramatically: I lost three stone in weight; I came out of a deep depression; I took up songwriting; I wrote my first book about the experience; and I went from being unemployed (and I thought unemployable) to being a full-time TV presenter and magazine columnist around the world.

Soul groups or soul clans

A soul group or clan is a group of souls who come back together in various lifetimes in order to support each other, or to create a set of circumstances for the good of one, some or all of the group members. A soul clan is a type of family, and just like a perfect earthly family, they will stand together in times of trouble. It's just that they are a family of the soul, rather than of blood. For instance, it's believed that many soldiers who died in the trenches, and undoubtedly had strong connections to their comrades, banded together to come back as peace protestors in the 1960s.

Soul groups or clans are the starting points for all past-life soul mates. A soul group consists of all the souls you've ever connected with in any amount of lifetimes. This doesn't mean every person you ever met in every life, because if you consider how many people you've already met in your current lifetime, and multiply that by the average amount of past lives people have, which is anything from five to five hundred, this would quickly become a totally unmanageable number. I'm talking about souls that have had an impact on each lifetime you've had. This is still a large number though.

You will, of course, have encountered some of those souls in your current lifetime because you will have become friends on the spiritual plane, whatever interaction you've had in physical lifetimes. They will be familiar to you, and familiarity brings comfort. We all need the co-operation of close friends and it's very likely that you'll have agreed to work with members of your group before you were born this time. Sometimes this co-operation will be during happy circumstances and sometimes it will be during difficult times. Members of your soul group often come through in the same life as you as Teacher soul mates to make sure you learn a necessary lesson. Sometimes a group will be brought together at once – this often happens with people who sit in a meditation group or circle. After a while, everyone who needs to be in the circle will have arrived and they will become established as a solid group. Quite often at this point, a meditation will reveal that the group are a soul clan and further investigation will reveal that there is something they are 'contracted' to achieve and which they will do very much as a team.

Soul groups or soul clans can include or even evolve into Twin souls, and can make wonderful partners. Or they can just be friends that feel like a family. Identifying your soul group is relatively easy. A lot of the time they will find you quite naturally. They might be the odd couple of school friends or work colleagues you stayed in touch with long after you left school or that job. They can be members of your blood family, and will be the ones who really seem to 'get' you. They might be long-lost friends who magically seem to come back into your life. Or you might meet them in a meditation group, or church, or any social gathering that becomes a regular fixture in your life.

Kelly's story

I recently had a past-life reading with Madeleine Walker, whom I contacted on your recommendation as I was puzzled about a recurring dream I was having about my daughter's father, whom I'm no longer with. It turned out that he and I had shared previous lives, the most prominent of which was in Northern Spain, where we lived on a Romany gypsy settlement.

Madeleine told me that I was a beautiful dancer, whose moves were so mesmerising that I was used to lure rich men into the camp, where they'd be robbed or worse. I fell in love with a fellow gypsy, and we married and had a daughter, but when a robbery went wrong and the victim was murdered, my husband (who is my daughter's father in this life), ran away with the others who were responsible. I pined for him and never got over him. I then became ill and eventually died of cancer of the uterus, and my daughter was looked after and raised by a group of kind women on the settlement.

When my daughter was born in this life, I'd already parted from her father, so I was on my own. From the moment she was born, I had an overwhelming terror that I was going to die of some form of cancer, and that she would be brought up by someone else and would not know me, although I could never explain this fear. I've also always dreaded dancing in public in this life – again, something I could never explain. I've always felt that everyone is staring and judging and that something bad is going to happen.

Madeleine explained that the group of kind ladies who raised my daughter in the previous life, were all part of my soul group, and some of them form my family in this life. I believe that my daughter's father is a soul mate, and I feel that my encounter with him in this life was meant to teach me a lesson, and that he agreed to do what he did in this life in order to heal me over what happened in the past life. Before the reading I felt very bitter towards him for not being there for our daughter and for me, but I now feel completely different and realise that this lifetime is but a short journey. He was in our lives for a reason, he was not meant to stay and I really feel that I've been able to move on since. The dreams have also stopped.

I now believe that we have multiple soul mates as part of a soul group and the reading with Madeleine also taught me that soul mates are not necessarily love matches or the love of our lives. They are so many different things, and it showed me that soul mates show us love on a completely different level from that we conventionally think of as love. They love us enough to help us in ways that we do not always understand, but which, ultimately, benefit our soul immensely.

I'd add to this by saying that sometimes soul mates that are other than Eternal Flames might come back to us in order to create a specific child, and that once that's accomplished they leave so that our true Eternal Flame can come along. Kelly blamed her death in the past life on her husband, believing that his running away had caused her to become ill, and, consequently, separated from her child. In this life, therefore, her husband had to help her recreate that same child, so reuniting mother and daughter on the earth plane once more.

Finding your soul mate isn't always simple

Almost all people who find a soul mate have known them before in previous lives. The only exception to this is if your soul mate is a 'new soul' and is therefore on their first incarnation. If this is the case and the soul has not been on earth before, then you won't have shared a past life with them and you won't recognise them – at least not at first – in their human form.

People tend to think that recognition of a past-life soul mate is always instantaneous, a sort of love-at-first-sight feeling, but the signs that you've known your partner before can be myriad and confusing.

While it can sometimes be instantaneous with Eternal Flames, this is by no means always the case. Sometimes it can take weeks, months or even years for the relationship to be truly understood. In those cases it takes that time because circumstances aren't right yet, and deep inside their souls, both parties have the maturity to be patient that comes with many lives and many relationships with that same person.

But one thing there *always* is 100 per cent of the time is a feeling of 'knowing'. This knowing feels like comfort and security: you feel safe with this person; conversation is easy; it doesn't feel competitive, just comfortable and reassuring. You can talk to this person from the outset without uncomfortable silences and with no need for small talk because you can tell them anything. There is also often recognition in the eyes. (That was certainly the case when I saw Garth Brooks. He does look quite similar to Ryan in a lot of ways, but it was the eyes that really gave it away.) Sometimes there will be an instant chemistry between the two of you, but quite often the relationship is first perceived as a wonderful friendship. I think most people understand that an enduring partnership will always bring deep and trusting friendship, whether the relationship is of a sexual nature of not. Successful marriages always mean that the couple have a strong friendship because only this can last through the years and keep them together through both trouble and joy.

If you feel you may have known your partner in a past life because you feel so relaxed and safe in their company, the one certain way of finding out is for both of you to be hypnotised. This should be done on the same day, but separately, so that neither one of you knows or hears what the other has recalled before being regressed yourself. If the same life is recalled by you both, then you have absolute proof that you are recalling a genuine past life.

If you do have a soul-mate relationship with anyone – your

partner, a relative, a friend, even a pet – then you can be sure that you will see them again, whether in spirit after you have both died or when one of you dies and chooses to come back in a new body.

Once you have met your soul mate and started a relationship, any minor difficulties there might be between you can often be resolved by finding out how you knew each other before, and whether there are any residual issues from that life that are hindering the progress of your current relationship from progressing smoothly, or as quickly as it might do otherwise. If you don't remember your soul mate from before, this needn't be an insurmountable problem. It just means that there might be things you don't fully understand about your relationship, or which you might have to find out through new experiences you share in this life.

Past-life issues can be very complicated. Even if you already know about a life you spent with a soul mate of any kind, it's a good idea to have regression under hypnosis with a therapist because they can ask the questions you want answered. If you're nervous about doing this, don't worry because an experienced past-life therapist will never plant ideas in your mind, but will simply allow your subconscious to come forward and speak freely (see Resources, p. 193 for more information).

CHAPTER 4

Oops, I Did It Again

Sometimes past lives can actually interfere with current lives and create a cycle of repetitive mistakes, resulting in unhappiness. In this chapter I'll help you unravel these situations and give you a clear understanding of how you and your soul mate can stop that cycle and get off.

Your soul mate's connection to you can change from life to life, even in the case of Eternal Flames. They can be your lifelong partner in one life, then come together with you just temporarily to help you sort out a problem or nudge you back on track. This is the proof of real love. They will still be your Eternal Flame because they are exactly that – eternal – but you may have agreed not to be partners this time round and to help each other in different ways instead.

This can cause its own problems because while we're in spirit, before we're born, the challenge we set ourselves appears readily 'do-able', but once we get here and grow up, it can seem an impossible task. Imagine for instance that in a past life you were sexual partners, but in this life you're brother and sister, or the same sex, or one is much older than the other, as in Nancy's story (see p. 45–47). The soul doesn't feel the same pull to obey convention as does the part of us that is mortal human and the attraction towards the other person is just as strong, whatever the circumstances.

Maggie's story gives us two examples of the ways in which past-life soul mates can make things go wrong in this life. The first involves a past-life connection she isn't meant to be with this time, and the second is an example of an ongoing connection over many lives that still has them trying to resolve old issues.

♡♡ Maggie's story

I have had two amazing soul-mate connections in my life.

The first was when I was fifteen. We came to Australia and were placed in Fairbridge Farm (a school where orphans were sent, which was eventually exposed for cruelty) until our parents could get settled. To cut a long story short, we left Fairbridge, our family headed for Kalgoorlie and I ran away from home. I was placed with a wonderful foster family but when my foster mother was diagnosed with a brain tumour she arranged for me to return to Fairbridge. It was an absolutely unheard-of situation. I just did not fit the picture.

There I met a lovely young man, called David, and we became firm friends. At times we were both lectured on how not to push things in the wrong direction, although two more innocent beings you could never meet; we had absolutely no clue as to what it was we were being told not to do. Anyway, there was an end-of-year fancy-dress dance and David turned up in an old army uniform, while I was in an old-fashioned dress. The moment I walked in to the hall and saw David my mind was flooded with memories. I saw us as another couple in another time, dancing the night away, scared and hanging on to each other. I knew that back then he was going away the next day and that I never saw him again. We danced all night – just as that other couple had done – and we wept tears for both of us. The minders interrupted a few times. They were in panic mode, but we were in another reality where he was heading for France never to return. I saw us at a train station, him tall and strong, shedding a single tear, me (her), trying to be brave, but collapsing in tears as the train left.

Two days later I received a message saying I was to leave the school and head home to Kalgoorlie. This time it was me who left on the train, and I never heard from David again, as my parents thought it best we did not get in contact. All his letters were burned, and mine never sent.

A few years later when I was married, I was shopping in Coles in Kalgoorlie with my son in a pram, when I came face to face with David. He said nothing – just stood there with tears running down his face, and I had to walk away. I couldn't speak and I have never heard of or from him since.

My second story involves a past-life reading I had done in which I was shown an image of a lady who was a priestess. She'd come from another place to what I felt was somewhere in Scotland. Because of her path of teaching and healing, her daughter's upbringing was left to her husband, a most unusual role for a man at the time, and one I was sure he would have been teased over. I saw him cooking over a fire – just the back of him – but the shock of curls and bushy hairdo stayed with me. I saw the priestess (my past-life persona) walk away. Her husband would not turn and watch her (me) go. I knew we'd argued many times about this decision. Next, I saw what appeared to be a wave of red and I was on an island with many others. Sunlight shone and bounced off shields. Somehow, I knew I'd died there.

Now in this life I met John. He's from Scotland, but for many years we've often been in the same places without ever actually meeting. I left Fairbridge months before he arrived there, for instance. He lived at the top of a hill in south Perth and I lived at the bottom. He lived around the corner from me in Langford – at the same time in both places. We discovered we'd been at the same events throughout the years and still never met.

In December 1989 I decided, for some unknown reason, to get work as a barmaid and I approached a friend who owned the then only Irish pub in Perth – The Briar Patch.

On my first night there, in walked John. The connection was electric, but I ignored it. He stayed to help clean up and then appeared every shift I worked. Apparently, the boys in the bar had a bet running to see how long it would take us to get together. I had this 'I-know-you' thing happening, but put it down to the things we had in common. After six weeks the bet was won and we were together. Then a dear friend showed me a picture of John in his soccer days, with curly, bushy hair, and it hit me like a thunder bolt that he was the same man I'd known in my past-life vision. A few years later we took on the guardianship of my two-year-old granddaughter (from my previous marriage), which turned out to be permanent. John stayed home and got her sorted for school and did the cooking, cleaning and caring, while I was on the road for my work as a psychic medium – and he still takes care of her today, while I travel.

Yes, we have had a few issues around his fear of me leaving and not coming back. Yes, we have had drama with the little one, but through it all, I know this is my turn to get it right. To understand the love and commitment he had in the past and has in this life. I feel this is my journey to learn his worth, and to be grateful that in both lives I've had someone who loves me deeply enough to assist me on my journey, which includes travelling to teach and assist others.

Sibling/family relationship

As mentioned above, a soul-mate connection can prove extremely complicated in a lifetime where Eternal Flame or Twin soul mates come back as siblings. This can result in two siblings being irresistibly drawn to one another, which can have disastrous results for all concerned.

Why would this happen? Why would we choose (if you believe we do choose our lives) to come back in such difficult circumstances? Like I said, when we are in spirit a challenge may not seem too great because from the place we are in we can see the whole story and not just the emotional human part, so we accept it as a means to some sort of end. Once we're here in the human reality, however, things are often very much harder than we anticipated. In these circumstances, I often suggest that the two people involved have past-life regression because understanding what went before can often reveal the reason for the problem this time, and this, in turn, can 'switch off' their need to be together as a couple – at least enough for them to function without it. It can be very compelling if both parties have the regression at the same time, but apart, so that when the life they recall turns out to be the same one they have immediate proof that they're experiencing genuine memories.

♡♡ Benny's story

I can't give my real name because my family never knew what my sister Penny and I went through.

We were always close, and being the older brother I always looked after her in school. It wasn't until she was sixteen and started to think about dating that we both realised things between us were not 'normal'. I just couldn't stand the thought of her with another boy, and I'd never even considered dating anyone myself. Penny is my other half and I am hers, and we soon found out that neither of us wanted anyone else. We never slept together I hasten to add, but we came close and we wanted to. We used to fantasise about running away to where no one knew us and living together as husband and wife. We knew we could never have children, but we thought it would have been worth it.

In the end, we couldn't do it; we couldn't just leave our parents never knowing what had happened to us, especially after our little sister died from meningitis, leaving them heartbroken. We both forced ourselves to date and each of us found someone and married and had children. I wonder what might happen when our parents die though because I still want to be with Penny.

I have tried to persuade Benny and Penny to try past-life regression to see why they feel the way they do about each other, but even if they do it might be too late to change the dynamic between them. They're reluctant to try it because they feel that to remember why they feel as they do will be a betrayal of their secret love for each other. To them, it would be as if they're denying a very strong love.

The sad thing is that both of them might be missing out on the Teacher or Comforter relationships they were meant to have this time round with soul mates they've never met because they grabbed the first people they could marry quickly to divert suspicion away from them.

Benny and Penny may well be Eternal Flames who have chosen to come back into this difficult situation this time. Or they might find that, in fact, they are only Twin soul mates and that their real Eternal Flames are out there somewhere, undiscovered, and might remain so if they don't break the past-life tie that binds them together and prevents them from opening their feelings to other people.

Same-sex relationships

Luckily, in this day and age being gay is nothing to hide in civilised company, and homosexuality is becoming increasingly accepted as just another demonstration of one person loving another. Past lives can confuse people sometimes because their subconscious remembers an altogether different scenario from the one they encounter in this lifetime and this can lead to a sudden change in sexual orientation.

Imagine someone who has appeared to be straight all their lives – totally and convincingly only wanting to be with the opposite sex and generating certain expectations from their families and for themselves. Then they meet a certain someone of the same sex, and suddenly, just like that, a homosexual relationship is apparently inevitable. They may well never be attracted to anyone else of the same gender as themselves again – but this is not about gender, because souls are not constrained by this. It's a soul-level love and, as such, it's inescapable.

This couple will find that they were partners in a past life, deeply in love on a soul level, and they will be unable to resist the pull of their attraction to each other, despite what convention may have drummed into them. Or their story might be slightly more unusual as this one is:

♡♡ Cassie's story

I've always thought of myself as being totally straight. I think I may even have been a little prejudiced towards gay people. But I never gave a thought to how they might feel.

I'd always thought I'd get married and have children and be 'normal' – whatever that is! My family expected that of me too. I'd always been popular, always had plenty of boys wanting to date me. It seemed likely that I would fulfil all of our expectations.

Then I met Carmen. She was dark, Spanish, exotic. I was blonde, blue-eyed, Scandinavian, cool. I couldn't believe how attracted I was to her instantly. It was irresistible, like I was carried along on a wave. I can still remember my poor mother's face a few weeks later, when I brought Carmen home and introduced as 'the person I love and want to marry'. To be honest, I know it was a harsh way to handle it, but I didn't know any other way. I just wanted to get it over with. My father went nuts – partly, I think, because he saw my mother's hopes and dreams crumbling. It only made us all the more determined though.

Carmen was my soul mate. I was totally sure of it, but life became quite difficult. We suddenly had to get our own place and pay for all our bills. Carmen's family were far away and couldn't have helped, even if they'd wanted to. My parents saw her as some sort of scarlet lesbian, determined to 'turn' their daughter, who had been perfectly 'normal' up until then. Anyway, we persevered and, in time, they did see some good in her. Mum was still sad about it, but she didn't spew hatred any more.

Then it all changed again. I went to see a psychic, just for a laugh, and she started to tell me about a past life of mine. I just giggled at first – it was all so silly. But then it started to make sense and my heart sank. She told me I'd once been my girlfriend's father. (I had not told her I was in a gay relationship.) She explained that my daughter back then was gay too, and that, as her father, I'd been draconian about it to the extent that she had killed herself. She said I had come back to be taught by Carmen that being gay was not a sin, and to be forgiven by her for driving her to suicide. I was staggered and my head reeled. Suddenly, I didn't know what to think because it all felt very true and real.

I put off going home to Carmen, afraid of what I might feel when I saw her. Would I see a lover or a daughter? I needn't have worried though because when I finally did go home she'd already gone. She'd packed her bags and left. There was a note from her saying that she was sorry, that she did love me, but that she needed to go. And at the end of the note she'd written: 'I forgive you.'

So in this case, Cassie and Carmen had known each other in a previous lifetime, and Cassie had mistaken the love (and guilt) that she had felt for her one-time daughter for sexual love with Carmen in this life. Carmen had come back as a Teacher soul mate. She certainly made Cassie understand how wrong she'd been in her prejudice, and made her understand that love is love, and, as such, it really is and should be the only thing that is ever-lasting and real.

Big age gaps

In some cases of past-life soul mates, a young girl might be attracted to a much older man or vice versa. But as with gender, souls know nothing about age because they are ageless. Love of this kind simply knows no boundaries. In the following account past-life regression proved unnecessary for the two people involved to understand what caused their dilemma.

♡♡ Carol's story

When I reached the age of thirty something very odd happened to me. I met a man called Carl, who was aged sixty-eight and I fell instantly head-over-heels in love with him. Carl was a very rich man and I was penniless, so his family made the obvious assumption and decided that I was a gold-digger. Much to my astonishment and dismay, my own family were horrified too. They thought I was trying to deny my roots and was embarrassed by them. They kept telling me that I was giving up the possibility of having a family of my own, and I knew they were right because Carl was not able to father children by then; and in any case, any child we could have had would have lost out on the joy of having a dad who could interact fully with them. I also knew that I'd end up alone, but I wasn't prepared to give up whatever time we would have together.

I tried to appease Carl's family by saying I'd sign a prenuptial agreement if we got married, but Carl wouldn't hear of it – he wanted me to be provided for. We struggled along for a while and we both started to have dreams of another life we'd spent together. We'd been an Indian man and woman, and I had been the man! It was very odd dreaming of myself as a man, and that was just one reason why I knew it had to be a memory, rather than just a dream. In the 'dreams' we discovered that I had married what was considered the wrong caste and our families had tried to tear us apart, just like they were now, only back then it was me (as the man) who had to stand up and defy them for love.

Today we are stronger than ever. Carl is eighty-seven this year and I dread the day we have to part, but at least I know we'll be together again in spirit.

In this instance, with family involved, regression or a dream wouldn't have been enough to change their minds, but perhaps, because the relationship has withstood the test of time, they will come to believe that Carol and Carl really are in love.

Some people, despite being considered too young for a relationship seem, in fact, to have maturity beyond their years because they are old souls who have lived many lives, often with the object of their affection. In the next story, the age gap between Megan and her older brother's friend was not so much the issue for her family as the stage at which they met. But with the passing of time, they could see that the 'puppy love' between them was genuine.

♡♡ Megan's story

My husband and I met under unusual circumstances. However, there was nothing unnatural about it. It's just not a typical story.

I met my now husband when I was eight years old. My brother is three years older than I am, and when we moved to the Hawaiian island of Maui, my husband became best friends with him. By junior high my parents began noticing that my brother's friend was hanging out with me more than my brother.

In my first week of high school we began dating. He said he would have officially pursued me sooner, but a 'high schooler' cannot date someone in junior high. Once he graduated from high school, he attended a local community college until I graduated. We then went to the same college in California together. We dated for seven years until we got married and will be celebrating our five-year anniversary in January. Looking back on our lives together, it was completely obvious that we were meant to be soul mates. Of course, when we met, we were naïve and didn't understand what soul mates are but, with hindsight, we wonder how it wasn't more obvious.

Luckily, because of their obvious past-life connection and the wisdom they gained from it, Megan and her husband's deep soul love was strong enough to give them the patience to wait until her parents considered her old enough in this life.

This next story is quite long, but I'm including it here in its entirety because it demonstrates very clearly how complicated soul-mate relationships can be. You can imagine how easy it would be, if you've had many different lives together and many different relationships with each other in those lives, to become confused and misunderstand what your relationship this time round is supposed to be.

♡♡Jim's story

Someone once told me that marriage for men comes in three stages. The first stage is primarily for sex, the second for love and the third for companionship. My first marriage was to a woman who I felt was beautiful and for whom I cared very much. It was her first marriage too, but it didn't last long and ended after about a year. I was crushed. I suppose many people go through their first divorce in much the same way, wondering what they did wrong and what was wrong with them. It took me a long while to recover from the pain, but my interest in women did not wane.

At the time I was living in a small New England town, working for a large IT company. I was still young and there were many attractive women at the office, so I played the field, so to speak.

Outside of work I met a woman a couple of years older than myself, whom I will call 'Gina', and something just clicked. She was certainly cute and attractive, but not in the way that was typical of 'my type'. But the appeal was more than just sexual. It was something that I had never quite felt before and certainly could not disregard. I also sensed that there was something special in the chemistry that was generated when we were in each other's company. She was already in a relationship and I did my best to respect that, but the pull was so strong that I couldn't just ignore her. Over time we found reasons to socialise together and we both knew that the attraction was gaining strength.

One weekend we both went to a barbecue at a mutual friend's house along with many others. At one point we found ourselves in a garden shed together and spontaneously got in each other's arms and kissed very passionately. Then she blushed, realising that her friends might notice and tell her boyfriend and so we spent the rest of the barbecue apart. We both knew though that we had to see each other again.

Soon after that I had a day off and she and I decided to go swimming at a local pond. The water was a bit cool as summer had not quite taken hold, but it was fun to jump in and enjoy the water. Gina joined me in the water with only her denim shorts on. I could hardly stand it. It was a chance for me to tell her that I loved her and not feel constrained in showing affection. My feelings for her were certainly physical, but also much more than that. I felt a true bond. It was as if we had lived and loved before in previous lives and had met again. I knew that she was my soul mate and that I wanted her with me for ever.

After that we saw a lot more of each other and she soon broke up with her boyfriend. Being with her was something that I always looked forward to. It was like reuniting with a lover after years of separation only the time frame might have actually been just a day.

My work took a good deal of my time, but I saw her whenever I had a spare moment. Anyone watching could tell just how connected we were to each other. From time to time my employment would require me to travel for a couple of weeks and each time I returned it was as if we renewed ourselves in our relationship.

Finally, my company requested that I move to another part of the state for a promotion. We were now separated by an hour's drive and although it was hard not to be able to see her on a daily basis, she would come to my place or I would travel to hers on the weekends.

Less than six months later the company asked me to move again to a neighbouring state for another promotion. This was getting hard. She helped me move again and we would still find ways to see each other on our free weekends, but we were now almost two hours apart in travelling time. To compound things, there was also the occasional out-of-town assignment where I would be gone for a couple of weeks.

One day Gina told me that she had been invited by a hot-air balloonist to go out for some balloon flights. I really couldn't blame her. I certainly was not around to keep her company and it sounded a fascinating offer. She would still meet me for weekends at my place and we would enjoy the strength of our chemistry.

Some time later, early one morning, we were woken from our bed by a very strange sound. It turned out to be some hot-air balloonists who were floating over my apartment and coming down in a nearby field. We got dressed and ran out to watch them land. It transpired that they knew Gina through her balloonist friend and the looks they gave me made it clear that she was more to this guy than just a girl he gave balloon rides to.

We had breakfast and talked. She told me that, yes she was seeing this guy and that she was torn between the two of us. It hurt me a great deal to listen, but I knew that I shouldn't have been surprised. When she was ready to head back home I asked her to spend some time thinking about making a decision between us. I felt that it was not fair to either of us for her not to.

When she left a huge emptiness filled my world. It seemed like I was shrinking and everything around me was pulling away. Later that night she called me. She had made up her mind. She would stay with the other guy. I felt everything drain out of me. All my life energy seemed to fall away. I was determined not to make things any more difficult though. I told her that I felt it was important that she knew who she loved more and wished her the best. But then she said that she loved me much more than the other guy. By now my head was spinning. I was so confused. I don't even remember ending the conversation. I just stood there in my apartment feeling lost and alone with nothing making any sense.

I don't suppose I was much use at work after that, but somehow I continued. My life felt so empty without her. It was like a conjoined twin had been ripped away from me. I had gone from feeling that I had found my true love, to being emptier than before I met her.

I spoke to her on the phone a while later. It was clear that she missed me as much as I did her, so she drove up to a town close to the border state where I met her and drove her to my apartment. We were so happy together at that moment. We could not get close enough to one another. I felt born again with her near me and this was reflected in our passion for each other.

We repeated this pattern over the months that followed until I was told I was going to be transferred once again. This time I would be a thousand miles away. I knew that this would mean a separation that would be the end of our connection. It was strange to be moving a step up in my career, but feeling that I was leaving my soul mate behind me for ever. To complicate things further, I was still dealing with the trauma of my original divorce. I was told it could take a full twenty-four months to get over the majority of the damage caused to one's psyche by a divorce and the calendar had still not turned over enough pages. My soul mate had pushed it all into the background, but now it was like a nagging monkey on my shoulder.

Since we could no longer meet with each other I would write to Gina from time to time. Her letters and cards meant so much to me. She would tell me of dreams she would have where I would be part of them, and I would think of her often. I could only hope that some day in the future we could be together again and I would feel complete once more. I hadn't lost interest in women and found opportunities to start relationships with several interesting girls, but no one really made me feel the way Gina did. There never was the chemistry and joining of spirits that she had generated in our relationship. These other women may have even sensed that they had some competition that they couldn't put their finger on.

Then came the day when I found another woman that I was very attracted to. While she wasn't a soul mate, I certainly was sincerely in love with her and we married and spent more than a decade together. Out of respect for my wife, I cut off my communications with my soul-mate girlfriend.

Thirteen years later I was single again for reasons that had nothing to do with my lost soul mate. My wife and I fell out of love, but still had respect for each other. With no extramarital affairs on our record, we called it quits. I never lost the longing for my soul mate though. I would wonder how her life was, what she was doing and where she was living. In one of her last letters to me she let me know that she had been asked to marry and had said yes to the same guy she had been dating when we had our first kiss at the barbecue.

A few more years passed and she would continue to come into my thoughts. On a whim, I looked up the phone number of her parents' home and called. Her sister answered, I told her who I was and asked her if she would be good enough to share my contact information with Gina. A couple of weeks later I received a letter from her. She had been thinking of me over the years. She continued to have dreams in which I would pop up. She was still married and loyal to her husband, yet we still yearned for contact and continued to write to each other. I let her know that truthfully, she was always in my thoughts and she expressed the same. She admitted that she had never lost her love for me.

I miss never having physical contact with my soul mate. It tears at me when I am in a part of the country near where she lives, but I also know that it would be a stupid thing to show up there. I do enjoy reading her letters, but I miss her voice, seeing her eyes sparkle and smelling her scent. I believe we really do have souls that are apart from our physical bodies and that we have lived before and probably will have another life after this. I believe that my soul mate and I have mingled in a previous life and it pains me not to have more time with her in this one. I don't think I would

have ever understood what a soul mate was if I hadn't met
Gina. I might have thought I did, but I never really would
have.

It's obvious that Gina was Jim's real Eternal Flame soul mate.
They are the ones we cannot lose or be unfaithful to, but as I have
mentioned, on the very odd occasion, they are not meant to be
with us in this lifetime. We're here to try and learn not to be too
dependent on each other, in order that our souls can develop to
their fullest potential or learn some other very important lesson.
Jim and Gina still maintain a connection though, because like I've
also said, this is a link that cannot be severed. The good news is
that having accepted their lesson, these two will undoubtedly
have a full relationship in another life. If Jim and Gina were to
have past-life regression under hypnosis, then they might discover why they contracted not to be together permanently this
time. Although the situation would still be painful, understanding the reasons behind it would make it easier to bear. Having
said that, occasionally when this kind of thing happens to give a
lesson to one or both parties, the very fact of understanding that
lesson can take away the need for it, and then, sometimes, the situation can change and they can be together, after all.

CHAPTER 5

Do Our Soul Mates Ever Really Leave Us?

People sometimes spend all the time they have with their soul mates worrying about losing them, whether through desertion or death. I want to reassure you that you can't actually lose a soul mate, and I'll explain why in this chapter.

People also wonder whether they can remain 'friends' with a soul mate if the intense relationship has failed, and I'll be covering that point too.

The loss of a soul mate through desertion is heartbreaking. You may be in shock because as far as you were concerned, there were no signs of a problem. The person you genuinely thought of as your soul mate may suddenly have given you a very poor excuse for leaving, usually along the lines of 'I need some space' or 'This isn't working out for me' and, when questioned, been unable to give a more concrete reason. It's as though they just have a gut feeling that they need to leave. This can even happen after marriage and the birth of children, which makes it even harder to take.

The big question you will be asking is 'Why?' and perhaps your greatest fear is that your chance of happiness has gone for ever. You may want to know how to win your partner back because you can't see a future without him or her. Or, if you accept their decision, you may then go on to torment yourself over either wanting to remain friends or resisting that suggestion. In the case of the former, you may tend to remain 'clingy', which often results in further trouble at some stage, which you are no better equipped to deal with. If you resist the idea of friendship, it may be because you feel too hurt and betrayed and also that you are now unloved by that person, which is often far from the truth.

Before I go any further, let me reassure you that if you find your one and only Eternal Flame, you will never really lose them, because you two are united on a soul level. Whatever happens on this plane, on this planet, in this lifetime, the bond you have cannot be broken, not by time, nor place, nor dimension. Ultimately, you will be together for ever, as having found you or been found by you, your Eternal Flame cannot live without you any more than you could exist without them. The only circumstance where you won't be constantly together is if you have contracted to be apart in order to learn something. But even if that happens, the connection, once made will be there throughout that life, and your Eternal Flame will still 'be there for you' and will come if you call.

Sometimes soul mates have to leave us when they pass away, but this is not for ever, nor is it a complete separation because every one of us leaves our angel base part in heaven at all times (see pp. 44–145); so if one person dies, they will return to the spirit world and be reunited there with their partner's angel base part. Even if this return is only temporary, and that soul returns to earth, the angel base part will still remain in heaven and be there ready to greet their partner (or any other loved one) when they die. Furthermore, if you're still alone, and think that in this life you won't ever meet your Eternal Flame, understand that you can at least still contact them. If, for whatever reason, this partner has decided not to come to earth at this time, you can still have their support, because you can speak to them through their angelic part. You can also use the method below to ask about your soul mates (see box).

How to speak to your angel

- Sit or lay quietly at a time when you won't be disturbed.

- Slow your breathing and close your eyes.

- Feel your way through your body from toe to scalp, and start to feel that you're walking in some beautiful place. This works really well if it's a place you've either been to or studied because you always wanted to go there.

- Listen and 'hear' the sounds associated with this place – the breeze in the trees or across the mountaintops, the birds or the sea, if you're on a beach.

- Lose yourself in the images of the place and see everything in as much detail as possible.

- Visualise somewhere lovely and peaceful to sit down, whether it's a grassy bank, a wildflower meadow, a fallen tree trunk or a comfortable sun lounger, then ▶

imagine your angel just sitting beside you, and simply ask the questions you want to, or ask to be able to speak to your Eternal Flame.

- Whatever you 'hear' or 'see' try and accept it with your intuitive right brain, and keep your logical left brain quiet. (The left brain is thought to handle all logical decisions – this is the part of your mind that insists on thinking about mundane issues or problems when you're trying to focus on reaching a meditative state. Your right brain is the part that gives you imagination and creativity and helps you to alter your mind state to one that's conducive to meditation.)

- Once you've discovered the information you sought, or you feel you want to return to the everyday world, thank your angel and count your breaths in your mind back from ten to one and, with each number, allow yourself to gently and gradually awaken from the meditation. Take your time and sit quietly for a while until you feel fully 'back'.

Even if you didn't reach your angel, you should still benefit from a feeling of relaxation and peace. And you can always try again – as many times as you like – because meditation is good for you.

Twin soul mates can, however, be a different story because sometimes they need to let us go as partners and that can be hard to accept as 'for the best'.

Alyssa's story below helps explain why this abandonment sometimes happens and what it may mean.

Alyssa's story

My husband Neil and I met in the card aisle of my local supermarket only hours after my boyfriend of three years had broken up with me. I'd only been back in the area for a few weeks after finishing my first year of medical school and was happy to be home. I'd spent that afternoon on the phone in tears because my ex-boyfriend's mother had called, saying, 'You guys can't break up . . . you're supposed to get married!' which made the split even harder. Later that evening, exhausted from an emotional day, I knew I had to get out and also needed groceries, so I threw on a pair of flip-flops and off I went to the supermarket.

Not two aisles into my excursion, I saw the card section and remembered Father's Day was just a couple of weeks away. I knew I had a busy few weeks ahead, so thought I'd be organised and started looking through the cards. But there were hardly any Father's Day cards left! That's weird, I thought. Maybe it's only me, because I don't usually buy a card until much nearer the day, but it was a little strange to me that everyone seemed to be really on the ball this year.

'Slim pickings, huh?' I heard from beside me. I'd been so intent on what I was doing and so mentally scattered from the day's events no doubt, that I hadn't even noticed someone had walked up beside me. Oh, good Lord, I thought. Of all the times to be picked up! I let out a polite laugh without so much as looking up, to try and send a message that I was not interested.

'Is it me, or is Father's Day like two weeks away?' he said.

Now I *had* to say something or I'd be flat-out rude. I turned to speak, but was totally unprepared for what was about to happen: as I looked up, our eyes met, and I quickly gave an awkward laugh and muttered an apology for my earlier rudeness. I wish I had a clip of what transpired next, but suffice to say that thirty minutes later we were still standing there, shopping trolleys side by side, and had somehow managed to get from A to Z with about a hundred things in common, one of them being running.

'Maybe you could give me your number and we could go running together some time?' he asked.

I left the supermarket that night with no clue as to what I'd actually purchased and not caring in the least. I remember thinking: what just happened? Even then, I knew it was something big and he hadn't even called yet. I returned home to find my sister's roommate, a friend of mine, sitting there. She looked surprised to see me returning from a trip to the supermarket with a smile on my face because I'd left with eyes swollen and red from crying.

'What took you so long?' she asked.

As I relayed my story, she commented, 'Only you Alyssa, only you.'

Neil and I married less than two years later on a lovely August evening in Sonoma, with just our families there. It was a magical night, when all was right in the world and the stars seemed to align just as they had that first night.

But as we embarked on our new life together, neither one of us could have imagined what we would be called on to walk through. Just shy of our fifth wedding anniversary I received the news that I was in Stage 4 of one of the rarest and most aggressive types of cancer known to man, and I was given less than a 1 per cent chance of survival.

What came next happened in a nightmarish blur: a total hysterectomy before we'd had any children of our own, gallons of high-dose chemo, two back-to-back bone-marrow transplants and almost a year of house arrest, while I went through the treatments and my immune system rebooted. And through it all, my husband, my best friend, loved me, and we loved each other through the tears at the thought of not being able to be together. We were just getting started, we were trying to start a family, we had so many things we wanted to do and see and yet, suddenly, we were facing the possibility of losing all of that in the blink of an eye.

But we made it – I made it and I made it because of him, for him. I couldn't leave him.

'You know I need you to stay, right?' he asked me one night in the middle of it all, when I was having a really tough time.

'Yes. Yes, I do,' was my answer.

And I need to stay to be with him just as much. He loved me when I was vibrant and healthy, when I was bald and broken and then when I turned into the person I am today. And once again, the stars have aligned and we celebrate our eighth wedding anniversary this August, more in love, and with a love that is deeper, wiser and stronger than ever before. Love really does conquer all.

If Alyssa had stayed with her first boyfriend thinking he was her Eternal Flame, there is a strong possibility that he wouldn't have been able to cope with what got thrown at them because he wasn't her true soul mate. He may well have collapsed under the strain of what happened later and his apparent love for her would have dissolved under the pressure.

That doesn't mean he was a bad person, just that Alyssa wasn't really his Eternal Flame soul mate in this life. He may well have been a Twin soul mate and needed to be with her for the period they were together, but something inside him made him move away at the right time. Had he not done so, Alyssa would most likely have avoided letting the encounter at the grocery shop progress. She would have been too wrapped up in her previous relationship to have considered talking for so long and so deeply to Neil, and he might well have walked out of her life, in which case she would never have had his unconditional love and unending support when she became ill, and she might not have recovered so amazingly – or at all. As it was, Neil was there when he was needed, to go through a terribly traumatic chain of events as Alyssa's rock, in the way that only a soul mate can do.

The next story, from Jude, illustrates once more that your true Eternal Flame soul mate might not be who you think it is, and a soul may be with you just for a specific reason.

Jude's Story

Ours was the perfect love story. Boy meets girl, falls in love, gets married, has children, a little cottage, picket fence, lives happily ever after. But here's where the record starts to scratch and jump and the story falls off the rails.

I loved Gemma from the moment I saw her, and she loved me too. I know she did. We both used to tell everyone that we were soul mates. We each knew what the other was thinking, often finished sentences for each other and answered unasked questions. Being together was so easy.

We had two little girls and I made a good living; we didn't really want for much. So you can imagine when, six years later, Gemma suddenly told me she was leaving I couldn't believe it at all. It seemed like a joke, but when I realised she was serious it seemed like a bad movie script. I kept asking why and she kept saying she didn't know why: she needed time, she needed to think, but she wanted us to stay friends. My first thought was, No! But for the girls' sakes I had to agree. I asked if there was someone else, but she said there wasn't.

I spent weeks trying to understand, while she was trying to find somewhere new for her and the kids to live. In the end, and before I had time to accept it, she was gone. Then, eventually – because it was the only way for them to have a roof over their heads in the long term – I had to hand over the house as well.

I had nothing, absolutely nothing; I even thought about suicide. How could a soul mate treat someone that way? I waited for a new man to arrive on the scene with her, sure that she must have one tucked away, and thinking that then I'd be able to hate her. But no, she continued to be a mum to the girls, only without me.

Finally, at the end of my tether, I wrote to a psychic, hoping to find reasons why it had all happened. She told me that she believed Gemma had only been with me in order to create our two special babies, for they had important roles to fill in the world. She said that Gemma and I were soul mates, but of a different kind. I didn't know what she meant at first, but she explained that we were soul mates in another life, and only contracted to be together as partners in this life to recreate the children we had lost to disease in that previous life. She said that Gemma's subconscious mind had told her to leave, to step aside for my true this-life soul mate. I didn't know whether to believe it or not to be honest, but it did make me feel better. It gave me a reason.

After a few months, I felt a bit happier. I got used to visiting my kids and to living in a crummy bedsit, which was all I could afford, what with maintenance payments and everything. I was taking a walk one evening, just to pass the time and thinking about how I'd have been tucking the girls in and reading them a story about then, and at first I didn't notice the woman. She was sitting at the kerbside under a lamp post. Given that it was nearly dark and she was a woman alone I was a bit reluctant to speak to her. But I was concerned that something was wrong, so I stayed a few feet away and asked her if she was OK. She held up a shoe over her shoulder, without looking round. It had a wicked-looking stiletto heel that was snapped and dangling.

'Darned fashion!' she said and got to her feet, turning to look at me. Just like that, I was dumbstruck and, apparently, so was she. I looked into her eyes and she looked into mine. The moment went on and on. I started counting and was soon at twenty seconds, and still neither of us had blinked.

'Er . . .' I said eventually, articulately. 'Can I help you?'

'Oh I'm fine,' she said, 'barefoot is better than no foot!'

I smiled and we turned, quite naturally it seemed, to walk side by side. And we're still that way – side by side.

And now? Well, Samantha (that was her name) and I live in a house her parents gave us for a wedding present. We have a huge garden and a pool. The girls come and visit often and Gemma and I are really good friends. I love

Samantha in a completely different and more powerful way from the way I love Gemma. I never thought that could happen.

It's bizarre the way life works out.

This story demonstrates several things. The most important and the hardest thing for people to get their head round is that people who love them sometimes leave *because* they love them. Something inside tells them that their contract – whether it be to make certain children together or to teach each other something – has ended and that they need to move on in order to allow their partner to take the next path on their journey. Even though the parting often hurts them too and they don't understand why things are happening the way they are, they're nevertheless compelled to walk away.

In Jude's case, the contract was about the children, and the soul-level love that Gemma felt for him meant that she had to let him go. He needed to be with Samantha for the next part of the adventure. I'm sure that in time, if it's meant to be, then Gemma will find her true-life Eternal Flame soul mate too. Jude was able to come to some acceptance of the situation, and because of that he was open to the possibility of a small miracle happening one day, whereas if he'd still been with Gemma, he might have resisted contact with another woman. His love for Gemma has settled into a warm nostalgia, maybe just from this life, but maybe from a previous one as well, and he doesn't need her to be with him any more in order to feel good.

It also demonstrates that it *is* possible to be 'just friends' with a soul mate. They will always be someone you can rely on, even if you're not together; you may no longer live in each other's pocket, but you'll always be there for each other. This is because soul mates' souls are always connected and it's a connection that can't be broken.

People who break up with those who they thought were their Eternal Flame soul mates, but were actually their Twin soul mates, often ask if there's any hope that they can get back together. This is a tricky one, because someone who loves you – as a soul mate always does – won't want to hurt you and go on hurting you, so yes, it is possible, with perseverance, to cajole them into starting up the relationship again. Whether or not this is a wise move though is a more difficult question to answer. All soul mates can live happily together if they settle for what they had before, but if they were meant to be with someone else, there will always be that little thing missing. Of course, if they never experienced that little extra facet, they won't recognise it as such, but will just feel vaguely dissatisfied as the years pass.

My advice is that if someone you thought was an Eternal Flame soul mate inexplicably leaves you, they probably did the right thing, and unless fate takes a hand and constantly throws you back together, you should try to accept the parting and move on. Otherwise you might miss out on what could be the greatest experience there is – finding and being with your true Eternal Flame soul mate.

Now, what about the other side of the coin? Clare's story shows what happens from the perspective of the person who ends the relationship.

♡♡ Clare's story

I believe my ex-husband is my soul mate, even though he's now my ex.

Although we met in an unusual way, I later discovered that

we had previously been at many of the same events together, but obviously the chance of meeting wasn't quite right at those times. He lives in south Wales and at the time, seventeen years ago, I lived at home in Somerset.

I've always thought we were drawn together, and felt like I was here to share our oldest son with him, a child he asked me for on our first date! After my second son was born we broke up, as my feelings changed into a different sort of love. It almost felt like I'd achieved what I was meant to and it was OK to move on.

I recently found out from a friend in the past-life field that my ex-husband and I had, in fact, decided before being born that we would be together for a period of time in this life, and that we would also be blessed with the very same souls of the children we had lost in our past life through starvation.

I can't help but always love him unconditionally, even when he's mean, because I think it's only human nature for him to feel inner anger sometimes at the failure of our relationship – and to show it! He's my soul mate.

Clare's pragmatic approach to what I believe was her Twin soul mate, rather than her Eternal Flame, shows that she did the right thing. The need to break up with him was overwhelming, even though at the time she didn't really have a good reason for it. Her ex will find his real Eternal Flame soul mate now, and perhaps Clare will too.

In yet another scenario, Jeryl's story shows that if your Eternal Flame is on the earth plane at the same time as you, fate will be persistent in bringing you together. Even if your soul mate appears to dash in and out of your life for years, they'll always be there on the periphery, ready to step back in for good when the timing is finally right.

♡♡ Jeryl's story

My husband Steve and I met when my ex-best friend introduced me to the man she was going to marry. She told me the two of them had so much in common that meeting him was like meeting me. We hit it off and had a lot in common but we were just friends. They got married and moved out of state.

They lived in Texas for about ten years. During those years, I was still friends with both of them. However, I didn't speak to them much, and when I did, I mostly spoke to her. She seemed to sense that there was always a spark between Steve and me, even though there had never been anything more than friendship between us. She didn't let me speak to him much. I think I spoke to him about once a year to wish him a happy birthday. I also saw him twice during those years: once, when I went to visit them in Texas for a week, the other time when Steve was on a business trip and surprised me by showing up on my birthday. He joined my family and me for dinner, along with a mutual friend of ours, Maggie, who had actually introduced Steve to his wife.

Steve and his wife decided to move back to the east coast since both of their families were there. Steve got a job in Massachusetts. He moved, and she stayed behind to sell the house. Maggie and I found out that she was meeting men on the internet. We felt bad, but didn't think it was our place to say anything because we had originally been her friend. Eventually, Steve found out anyway, and they split up. Steve was still living in Massachusetts then, but he had no family there, and he was lonely. He started coming down a lot to visit my family and me in New Jersey on weekends. We really enjoyed hanging out together, but we were still just friends.

Steve then had to go to Texas to settle the divorce and issues involving custody of their three-year-old son. While he was gone, I missed him more than I thought I would. One morning, I woke up and just knew that I loved him and that I didn't want to be without him. My father spoke to Steve in Texas and told me later that Steve had said he loved me. When Steve called me himself, I asked him what he meant by 'love'. Not knowing how I felt about him and not wanting to get hurt, Steve was evasive. However, by the end of the conversation we both knew that our feelings for each other were more than friendship.

Steve ended up getting custody of his son. He moved to Maryland to be near his family. His son went to Florida to spend some time with his grandparents while Steve got settled. During that time, he came up to New Jersey and surprised me again. We went on our first official date. From that moment, both of us knew we would be together always. We were engaged about eight months later and married just under a year after that. We have now been together for fourteen years and married for twelve of them, and we have two daughters.

When a soul mate dies, the remaining one can sometimes feel betrayed in just the same way as one who has been deserted. This was the case with Steven, who wrote to me after his wife died.

♡♡ Steven's story

Soul mates are for life, aren't they? Then why did Stella die and leave me? She always promised me she would never leave me, and yet she had a car crash and was killed. Why wasn't she protected? Why wasn't she more careful? How could she be so careless with my love and dreams for the future? Why wasn't she saved? We'd found each other and, to me, that meant we'd grow old together. I feel cheated.

When the police came to my work to tell me about the accident, at first I just didn't believe them. I thought they'd made a mistake. It couldn't be Stella. It couldn't be my soul mate. We were going on holiday, and that's what I told them over and over. It couldn't be her because she'd been looking forward to the holiday.

Stella and I met when we both started work right after school, but the time hadn't been right for us, and after a couple of months she left to take a better job. Then, ten years later – just two years ago – we met again, quite by chance at a fairground. I took her on the dodgems and she screamed in mock fear and clung to me. It felt so good and right then that I was determined to marry her. We got married eighteen months ago, and now she's gone. Just like that.

This is a heartbreaking scenario. There are so many lonely people in the world, desperately searching for someone, and here was a couple who on the face of it had succeeded in finding their one perfect mate.

So what explanation could there be for this apparent, if unintentional, abandonment? Hard though it will be for Steven to accept, there is a much bigger picture going on here than he can see right in front of him. Each and every soul on the planet came here for a purpose. Not only that, but they are also on a journey for the progress of their own soul and spirit, and sometimes that means things have to happen that don't make us happy in this lifetime.

When we love someone – truly love them – the kindest thing we can do for them after they've passed is to progress with our lives and let them go. We don't have to let go of the love – not at all – but we do have to try and let go of the pain. This is for their sake, in that they wouldn't want their passing to knock us right off track in our own development, and they need to be free to move forward into their next life, which may even include them coming back here in a new body. This is what has sometimes happened when you find a very young person falling in love with a much older one. (Sometimes one soul will come back much quicker than the other, and so end up in a completely different generation. The age gap won't prevent the two soul mates from wanting a relationship though.) It can also explain how someone who's been straight all their lives can suddenly fall helplessly in love with someone of the same gender. This kind of apparently mismatched love happens sometimes because the partner who was lost in a previous life comes back into the world with a completely different agenda and priorities from those they had in their previous life, or they might be male when they were once female or vice versa.

So what can Steven do in this case? He can let Stella go with love and forgive her for leaving him. He can rest assured that he will be with her again in some form at some time, and that he will always have a part of her in his soul. Who knows what the future may bring for him. He must also have faith in their connection.

Everyone who has a soul mate in their lives knows that it's a connection that can't be severed. In time, he'll see the bigger picture and understand why they were together for just the time they were.

Stella will very likely direct Steven to someone who can be there for him and comfort him. This is another reason why soul mates often surprise people by first of all claiming they can't live without their partner, and then very soon after that starting a relationship with someone new – sometimes even their partner's carer or nurse. This is because that nurse was often chosen by the dying soul mate because he or she knew that they would be the right person to kickstart their partner into new life and give them new energy.

On the other hand, as Paula's story demonstrates (below), sometimes there is just the one soul mate, and when they are your Eternal Flame and they die, there is no one to take their place. Once you've had the love of a true Eternal Flame soul mate, you can't be satisfied with anything less.

Paula's story

I'm a widow, and my husband of thirty-five years transitioned (died) on 26 April 2005. We were high-school sweethearts, lovers and best friends. I truly believe that he was my soul mate. Do I think that we have more than one soul mate? My answer at the present time would be, no. And I would like to add that I have nothing to base my answer on other than what I feel deep within my very being, deep within my heart and soul.

I guess I felt our connection at a soul level. I felt that I could never say goodbye to him. We dated in high school and then I went away to college and Eddie was drafted into the army. We stayed in touch and we went out whenever he came home on leave. Our friendship turned into love. Before he asked me to marry him I just knew that I could never say goodbye to him (whether he had asked me to marry him or not – there was just something there, some soulful connection, some indescribable energy between us). I just knew that we were meant to be together – there was a strong, spiritual bond.

After his sudden death I was so lost and alone, grief washed over me with an unrelenting force and magnitude. I searched for answers. I read everything that I could on death and dying. I cried out to God. I told him that he had it all wrong; I told him that I needed to know Eddie was all right, I told him that I would be all right if I could just stay connected to him. And, God answered me: Eddie and I are still spiritually connected.

I'm a writer and I've written a book, *From Death to Living in the Light* as a result of my walking through the valley of the shadow of death with my husband. It contains my conversations with God, and the spiritual visions that I had before my husband died, as well as the after-death communications that I have received. Needless to say, it hasn't been published – perhaps it was only meant to help me on my spiritual/healing journey. However, that's beside the point. The point I am getting to is that I feel that we stay connected with our soul mate throughout eternity. I couldn't say goodbye to Eddie in life, and I still cannot say goodbye to him while he is in his spiritual form.

I do believe that we are all here in our physical form to learn certain lessons. Perhaps as soul mates one of the

lessons that Eddie and I were here to lear
could stay connected after death – that love is the
that matters, and that love is what keeps us connecte
is the energy/force of all things.

In Paula's case her husband and Eternal Flame soul mate, Eddie, actually communicated to her after his death to affirm her feeling that death could not part them. As I said, soul mates can never really be parted – it's just a question of reaching out and accepting that touch from someone who is, in reality, only a breath away.

Leave Us?

was that we

only thing

d – it

101

CHAPTER 6

'...dences' and
Magical Notions

I'm a firm believer in the power of synchronicity – a term coined by the well-known Swiss psychologist, Carl Jung, to describe a series of events that seem to come together to form something meaningful to you. These strings of coincidences can often appear random and mysterious and may not make sense at first, but those of us who do take heed and follow them come to see an actionable pattern and totally believe they can have a meaningful effect on us through the message they bring. I am convinced that there are very few pure coincidences in this world and my philosophy is that if you've asked a specific question and you get a sign that appears to present an answer, then it probably is one.

In this chapter I'll be exploring the types of signs which lead you to your soul mate, and I'll also be tackling the connected subject of spirit guides (souls that were once human and, having passed over, have elected to maintain contact with us in order to help and guide us – see p. 113) and whether or not they can be soul mates too.

Can an apparent 'coincidence' help you decipher a path to your soul mate?

My experience has shown that we are constantly given signs in order to smooth our paths. The trick is learning to spot them and take notice. It's a bit like when you get a new car, and suddenly, the same make of car seems to be everywhere you look, whereas you'd never noticed it before. So it is with these signs – once you become aware of them, you see them very easily and wonder how it was that you used to miss them.

You can call the bringers of these signs or messages angels, guides, your higher self, intuition or your imagination (which is just the creativity that comes from listening to your subconscious). In the end, it doesn't really matter where you think they come from, so long as you take notice of them – the key is to be open. So if you get signs that might appear coincidental, just try following them. You have nothing to lose and everything to gain by seeing what happens.

Signs can take many forms – here are some of them:

- You suddenly find yourself thinking of an old friend you haven't seen in years, and then you bump into them, or they call you. If this happens, pay close attention to what they say, as your message may be contained in their words.

- A certain number or sequence of numbers might keep appearing to you – for instance a clock or a calendar may show that number, and then a map reference is brought to your attention somehow and it contains the same number. You might wake up at that exact time. If this happens you can add the numbers together and perhaps consult an expert in numerology to see what the total means. Or you can start to look for the number and literally follow it. For instance, I know one person who followed her repeated numbers to a date and a time and an address. This led her to a church and to her future partner who was sitting in his car outside, looking for someone to give him directions. This led to a dinner date and, in time, a marriage.

- You might be driving along a familiar road when you suddenly get a feeling that you should go another way. Or perhaps you're walking, intending to go to a certain place, and your feet seem to want to go elsewhere. If this happens, you should follow your feelings because it may lead you to something unexpected and good.

- If you're trying to make a decision, stop stressing and going around in circles over it – just let go of it and see what happens. You might get a phone call or email that seems to give you an answer in a covert way. This is why some people use angel cards (a set of cards with angel portraits and a few words of angel wisdom on them) or even tarot – the seemingly random choices made when selecting a card may not be random at all.

- You might be trying to make a choice of some kind while listening to the radio, and a series of songs might come on, the lyrics of which seem to tell your story and then take you forward, 'telling' you what your decision should be.

- Someone you once had difficulties with might suddenly appear in your life again, only with the roles reversed so that this time, you might be the one with the power. If this happens, try not to take advantage of the situation, but think about what it might be trying to tell you instead. Listen to any clues in what they say to you when you discuss the past.

- Dreams can bring you messages, especially when you haven't been asleep for long enough to have gone into classic and well-understood REM (rapid eye movement) sleep or are rousing from sleep, but are not entirely conscious yet. The former is known as the hypnogogic state and the latter the hypnopompic state. Both are known as 'threshold consciousness' and can bring strange, sometimes prophetic dreams and no one really knows where they come from.

- Animals can bring you signs, perhaps through their behaviour or how many of them there are. Any unusual behaviour in particular must be noted.

Sometimes messages are like jigsaw puzzles and it might take many incidences to form a pattern that can be read and understood; other times they are as plain as day in their meanings. Take note of anything unusual, including dreams, because in time your scraps of notes may form one big, clear picture.

In the following stories the people involved share their accounts of the signs and 'coincidences' that led them along unorthodox routes to their soul mate. If they'd ignored their signs and feelings and hunches, they might have missed the opportunities presented to them. Donna and Diana (below) obviously recognised the 'soul-pull' of their soul mates, even if they didn't really understand what it was at the time, and both were intuitive and open enough to be led in the right direction.

♥♥Donna's story

I met my husband of thirty years in a very unconventional way. I'd been going to basketball games to support my local team for a few months and found myself watching one player as he came off the bench and played his three or four minutes. One night I watched an away game on TV and again I found myself watching this one player as he came off the bench. I heard the announcer mention that the team would be flying back in to town at midnight. Almost without thinking about it, I got dressed and drove twenty-five minutes to the airport where I waited for him to disembark. Then I asked if he would have lunch with me. The next day we went out to dinner instead and that was in 1978. We were married two and a half years later.

♥♥Diana's story

I met my soul mate when I was browsing a website for a summer-holiday apartment in the USA. In the search I stumbled across a very brief ad that read: 'Write to US inmates'. Almost without thinking, I responded with, 'I would be interested in corresponding with a US inmate. I am English and live in Spain. I will tell you more if you are interested.' I clicked and sent and thought no more of it until I received a response around one month later from the volunteer group who facilitated the exchange of correspondence between inmates and volunteers.

I received a letter of introduction from an inmate in a California prison. On reading it, I had a strange feeling – a kind of knowing. It's difficult to articulate the sensation that came over me, but as I said, it was a kind of knowing that my life was about to change dramatically.

Communication flowed easily between us and I soon found myself rushing every day after work to the PO Box I had set up to see if there was a letter from him. I was aware of the bond we had made so quickly, but it didn't occur to me immediately that I could be falling in love or that I had found my soul mate. I didn't want to entertain such thoughts, although I was aware that something was going on with my emotions. As our communication became more frequent and our friendship strengthened, I began to consider more seriously what might be occurring. After around five months of correspondence, he expressed his feelings towards me and by that point it felt as if we were destined to be together. Nevertheless, I hesitated before responding as I knew that by admitting my feelings I would be getting into a very complicated situation.

To cut a long story short, I told him that I felt the same way, and a short time after that we spoke for the first time on the phone. We then spent a few months communicating by both letter and phone. During one of our telephone conversations he asked me to marry him, and I accepted. Although I had never even met him in person at this point, nothing had ever felt so right to me in my life. I was forty-eight at the time and despite having had many relationships – some long-term – I had never believed those partners were my soul mates. I had always felt that there was something missing. But this time I didn't; I felt totally in sync with this man. Communication between us flowed, about anything and everything, and most important of all, we shared the same views on love, honour and loyalty.

I met him in person for the first time seven months after we started writing to each other. It was both the scariest and the most wonderful day of my life to date! We've been married for three and a half years now. I make the trip from Spain to see him every eight weeks or so. We speak around four times a week on the phone. He is my rock, my friend, my soul mate. We are able to rely on our spirituality to help us cope with not being able to be physically intimate. I feel 100 per cent connected to him, despite the distance between us and lack of opportunity for us to be together in the traditional sense. We often have telepathic experiences – uncanny in a way, but I believe we are connected via the cosmos. We can read each other like a book, despite having spent relatively few hours together in person. It's not easy to articulate such feelings, but it's as if there is a total oneness between us. I can't imagine finding another to whom I feel so connected.

Diana's story just goes to show how a simple sign, such as an advert flashing up on your computer screen, can lead you to your soul mate. The next story also demonstrates how chance happenings can do the same.

Mona's story

I've always been straight – or thought I was – and never imagined I would be attracted to another woman.

On 'that' magical day, I woke up and realised that I hadn't shut the curtains properly. Sunlight was streaming through the gap so brightly that I changed all my plans for working and decided to spend the day at the coast instead. I set off, only to discover that I was low on petrol. Feeling stingy for some reason, I refused to stop at a rural garage with its high prices and drove on fumes towards my destination. Of course, I ran out. As the car faltered, then ground to a halt, I cursed my stupidity.

Having been rescued by the AA, I decided it was too late for me to make it to the coast, so detoured instead back to a small village I'd liked the look of as I'd driven through it. There was a pub that seemed like a good bet for lunch, and a 'chance' conversation in the pub led me to a garden centre I'd never been to before.

I was standing there, admiring the roses, when a female voice beside me said, 'I just love to be given roses, don't you? By the right person though, of course.' I turned to face the source of the voice and my eyes locked with the most beautiful blue eyes I'd ever seen. I was mesmerised. I muttered something or other, a bit embarrassed to find myself strongly aroused by another woman. I hurried to the till and out to the car. I was fumbling with the lock when a single red rose appeared in my eye-line, quickly followed by those blue eyes and the incredible woman they belonged to.

The next hour was a blur. We went back inside, and although at first I was just a bit flattered at the unexpected interest, I was soon totally captivated by her and started saying silly things to prolong the afternoon. We ended up having dinner that night, and by midnight we were in bed together.

It was very strange, but also totally familiar somehow. My synchronistic journey led me to a partner I've now been with blissfully for ten years. I don't know who in the universe engineered my finding my Eternal Flame, but someone sure did.

Some people – like Allison below – demonstrate that even if you do miss the signs, all you do is delay the inevitable.

♡♡ Allison's story

When I think of a soul mate, I think of my parents. They've been together since they were teenagers and were high-school sweethearts. They dated for seven years, got married, waited seven years, had me, waited another seven years, then had my brother! Their lives just seemed to fit.

Growing up, I always had trouble finding a decent man to date. The boys where I lived were not serious and I always found myself in uncommitted relationships – that is, I was seriously involved with them, but it was never a two-way street. I often went to my mother, asking her advice as to what I should do. She told me that 'patience is a virtue' and that everything would fall into place when it was meant to. But as I went through one failed relationship after another it seemed as if the 'meant-to-be' part would never come.

I asked my mother how she'd met my father and how they'd made it work for so many years. I learned that she didn't like my father in the beginning and found him very annoying. But the love they now have for each other is timeless and truly from their souls – so he must have ended up doing something right! And I learned that I'd have to be a little more selective when it came to what I wanted in a man if I was going to find 'The One'.

Then on Halloween in 2009, I met Herbert. A mutual friend introduced us, but I found him really irritating at first. I was in one of my 'relationships' at the time and barely gave him the time of day.

Herbert was persistent though. He kept calling me and he asked me on dates. He even bought me a Christmas present one year. I found it odd that someone who hardly knew me could be so head-over-heels for me.

Our first date was ridiculous. He took me to a restaurant called Chilli's. I was twenty-one at the time and he was twenty and I didn't like the idea of dating a younger guy, even though there was only a year between us. He ordered a fruit punch with his meal and I remember thinking: I can't even take him to the bar with me.

I was picking him apart to the last detail because I think that deep down inside I knew that he was the one, and I was scared of that. When you are so used to being on a one-way street, in terms of relationships, the idea of real commitment is scary.

Needless to say, we went on a few more dates, but I wouldn't give up my 'uncommitted' relationship because I thought I was in love with that guy. I finally realised one day that I wasn't getting anywhere in that relationship, and when I broke it off I reconnected with Herbert, having not spoken to him for over six months.

Herbert accepted my apology for being so inconsiderate of his feelings and we agreed to start over and become friends. However, he was in a committed relationship by then and it was the wrong time for anything to happen between us. He said, 'I can't believe you had to do this now. It's too late,' but then he ended up breaking up with that girl because they had their own issues and we began dating.

Initially, I wanted things to get going right away, fearing that otherwise I'd end up in a yet another 'uncommitted' relationship, but Herbert now had his guard up, and wouldn't let it down for anything. But with time and a lot of effort on my part, he eventually realised that I was serious about giving us a chance. We've been dating ever since, and I know he's the one I'll marry and have babies with.

We've been through a lot in the time we have dated. His father recently passed away from cirrhosis of the liver and I stood beside Herbert through what was the most difficult time of his life. And strangely, when his father was dying and we were in the hospital with him, Herbert's mother told me the story of how she and his father had met. She said: 'Oh my goodness! He was so persistent and wouldn't stop bothering me.' I laughed and thought to myself, like father, like son! His mum assured me that, 'You know he's the one when you don't like him at first!' And she couldn't be more right. A few years ago, I couldn't stand him. Now, I can't imagine my life without him. He is my best friend, the love of my life and my soul mate!

It's unusual to dislike your soul mate at first sight and then grow to love them, but I honestly think that Allison had been hurt so many times that she shied away from the intensity of her feelings. She blocked them out and forced herself to believe that she didn't want Herbert. She was scared that she would lose out again, and that if she did, this time there would be no getting over it. (See pp. 123–124 for information on how hypnotherapy can help you unblock emotional barriers.)

These stories have helped to demonstrate that when we do follow the signs, things can happen very quickly; when we choose not to, although we still end up in the same place eventually, it takes us much longer to get there and we can waste a lot of time in the process.

Do some soul mates stay around us after death to be our guides?

Spirit guides are the souls of either animals or people who have passed over. They are always people and animals we knew in life, be it this one or a previous one (maybe even centuries ago) and with whom we had a soul-mate connection of some kind. Their love for us is such that they will stay anchored in the earth plane after they pass instead of progressing forward, just to help us.

Spirit guides steer us through our lives, help us to stay on our right path and, often, to find more soul mates. In this role, they are generally soul mates of the Teaching kind, supporting us through our learning experiences. They can be with us for the whole of the rest of our lives or they can be transient. I've had five guides so far. Sometimes, because they are friends to our souls, it can be hard to let them go, and some can even be persuaded to stay, but we have to try and remember that they do know what's best for us.

Delilah shares her story of one such relationship:

Delilah's story

I met Bill in 1974. He was a man who lived life on the edge. He'd lost all his family in a car accident in America, so he did drink and smoke, but he had a heart of gold and I fell madly in love with him.

Bill always told me that he was only going to live to be forty years old, but made a promise that he would come back after he died to let me know he was all right. The years went on and we had a daughter called Becky, but by then Bill's health was deteriorating through his continued smoking. I got up one morning in November 1988 to find him dead in a chair. He'd had a massive heart attack, and he'd just turned forty-one. My daughter was only eight years old and I was devastated.

The night before Bill's funeral I was in bed with my daughter lying asleep beside me. She was restless and kicking out, so I know I wasn't asleep. I felt myself rising up above my body, and I then saw a bright light – a green fluorescent ball.

I knew this light was Bill. The light and I began dancing around the room together like two joyous spirits that had found one another. I can't begin to describe the happiness and love I felt. Then our spirits merged and I truly knew what it was to be at one with someone. I can only tell you that this is what pure love feels like. We communicated telepathically and I was told not to worry because everything would be all right. I felt so calm and comforted and also ecstatically happy. I said: 'I'm OK now, you can go back.'

I felt myself slip gently back into my body and once again could feel my daughter moving restlessly beside me. I know this really happened and I knew from that moment on I had nothing to worry about and that Bill was still with me. In fact, he has made his presence known to me many times: I've smelled his aftershave and the lamps have flickered.

Bill's death sent me on a spiritual search which resulted in me becoming a past-life regression therapist. If he hadn't come back to guide me, I would never have gone down this path.

This next story is short, but is probably my favourite story in this book. It gave me goosebumps when I first read it, and I bet it will do the same to you.

Sarah's story

When I first met my now husband and soul mate, I was in a really bad way. We met at an event, and he gave me his number, but I was in such a bad place I threw it away. A few days later I had a dream, and in it a teenage boy came to me and told me I had to find the man again. I've never been so sure of the truth of anything in my life. I tried to find his number to no avail, then decided just to go back to a similar event the next month and hope he was there. He was.

When we met again he said to me, 'I knew you'd be here, and I'm going to marry you.' We got together and when I first visited his house I was stunned and surprised to find a picture in his room of the boy who had visited me in my dream. It was his fourteen-year-old son who had died a few years before in a car accident. I find it so touching that my husband's son's spirit went to so much trouble to bring us together.

Our daughter, who is now eleven years old, came into the house from outside the other day saying there was an angel at the bottom of the garden, called 'Spiffy'. I thought nothing of it until I told my hubby – it turns out that was his nickname for his son. I'm glad to know he's still with us and guiding us.

When people find themselves in need or they're alone and could do with a friend, they will often ask me how they can connect with this kind of soul mate. It's important that they can, because searching for one's Eternal Flame or life partner can be frustrating and make a person feel alone, so it's good to know that they can get help from a spirit who understands them. Luckily, getting a connection with this kind of adviser is quite easy. No matter how alone you are or how desperately you've been searching for a living human soul mate to share your life with – or if you've had a soul mate and lost them – you *will* find comfort in these celestial friends.

On very rare occasions an Eternal Flame will come back as a spirit guide. I haven't heard of many cases, but there are a few. I think it happens when the bereaved person finds it impossible to carry on without their partner, and there is a danger that they will fall off their rightful path if left alone. The only other time I've seen it happen is when the two souls have made a contract for it to be so before they were born this time.

How to meditate to make a connection with your spirit guide

Your mind is like a sponge and obediently stores everything you see, hear, read and experience – from life-changing events to soap operas, news programmes and even advertisements. But from a meditation point of view what you have to do is put your mind to one side and refuse, for at least a little while, to live in it. See it there, beside you and accept it, but say that for the next ten or fifteen minutes you are not going to exist in there. Rather, you are going to exist in the empty space right next to it.

Practice makes perfect

First make sure you're not going to be disturbed. This can be difficult if you have a family, but this practice of meditating is as important for your wellbeing as eating and drinking, so even setting aside just thirty minutes a week for it will be worthwhile.

Next, practise raising your hand and literally 'pushing' your mind to one side. If any issues pop out at you, just firmly push them back, saying you'll deal with them at another time. The more you do this, the better at it you will become. Once you feel you have a certain amount of control over the position of your mind and its separation from your spirit, you are ready to try to connect to your guide/soul mate:

- It's a good idea to have a focus, and one of the best is a live flame, such as a log fire, or failing that, a candle. Now take a few moments to think about what you're going to ask your guide. The most common question is, 'What is your name?' Make sure your intent is clear (to do this it's helpful to say something like: 'I am trying to connect with you so that you might help me be happier in a way that will be for the highest good of all involved').

- Sitting quietly, with your eyes focusing only on the flame, let your eyes go soft so that your brain can relax. Stroke one forearm with the other hand, softly and gently, as if comforting a child. Do this over and over until you feel very calm and relaxed.

▶

- Control your breathing, thinking consciously about every breath you take. Imagine you're breathing in the golden light of the flame with every inhale, and breathing out any smokiness within you as you exhale.

- After a while your mind will switch off and you'll float in a world very similar to that which you experience just before you go to sleep. Now just 'be' and listen. Whatever comes into your mind, accept it as the answer. Stay in this state for as long as you can.

- Try and 'see' your guide in your mind's eye. If you're sceptical, that's absolutely fine, as this practice can still help you on a physical level by encouraging you to relax and by reducing stress. And, in time, you may also come to see and hear things that you can believe in.

Using spirit guides and signs to find your soul mate

This story illustrates perfectly how to use your spirit guides and also follow the signs to find your soul mate. It's an astonishing story which should convince even the most hardened cynic of the validity of these spiritual messages and guides.

Barbara's story

When I was a little girl my home life wasn't good. No one understood me, and at school it was even worse. I was beaten, and on one occasion even stoned – all because I was 'different'.

Every night a feather-adorned, incredibly tall Native American man would stand at the foot of my bed. He told me he was my spirit guide, and that he was called Touch the Clouds. When I tried to tell my parents about him, they got angry. They thought I was either extremely naughty, making things up or possibly bonkers! But Touch the Clouds was my friend. He kept me sane through my difficult childhood.

All the time I was growing up I used to dream of going to the USA. I wanted to go where Touch the Clouds had once lived. I also thought that my soul mate would be waiting there. As soon as I could, I started the journey to find my beloved. I flew and drove to places that drew me. I'll always remember going into my first trading post. I headed straight to a card stand with pictures of Native American Indians from the 1880s. As I turned the stand around to view the other cards, there was Touch the Clouds, beaming from a postcard! In the artist's portrait he was standing tall and proud just as I'd seen him. I remember him touching the ceiling in my room because he was so tall, and here he was. On the back of the card I read, 'Touch-the-Clouds, Miniconjou leader, seven feet tall, cousin and friend of Crazy Horse'. I just couldn't stop crying. Any doubt that others had sown in my mind left me. I was free to believe without question that he was my gatekeeper, guardian, and spirit father.

At the beginning of 2006 I fell ill with a stroke and peritonitis and almost died. Just weeks after I recovered, Touch the Clouds told me I would find my 'heart mate' in Hawaii. I left Britain the next morning, telling many friends, without any doubt in my heart, that I was going to meet my husband. By obeying my guide's instructions I was literally going for broke. I'd always wanted to see a live volcano and I intended to stay that night at the bed and breakfast near Kilauea, but my spirit guide knew otherwise. Instead of going there directly, I inexplicably found myself in the car, driving further west. I didn't have a map with me, so just accepted that I was off on another magical mystery tour. I felt relaxed as my spirit patiently led me for the next two hours.

By late afternoon I was on my own, in a foreign country, miles from anywhere, just taking a leap of faith. Finally, I saw a turning just moments before I felt my body instinctively snap the car to the left and on to that road. I caught breathtaking glimpses of the ocean a few miles away as the winding road drew me ever closer to it.

There I found Dragonfly Ranch. At the top of the stairs leading to the door, was a well-tanned man, smiling expectantly at me. I ascended the steps breathlessly and stood in front of him. I looked into his eyes and saw myself. I gasped. Here was my beloved, my other half. I had come all this way to find him, and now I was home.

I found myself in his arms, and we both knew there was no more need to search. He was called David. Later that night, he told me that he'd known for some time that I was coming for him, from Old Europe. Like me, he'd never given up hope that his soul mate would join him in paradise. By our third day, we were staying together at the condo on Kauai. That romantic evening on our balcony, with whales crooning in the distance, he asked me to marry him.

I wept uncontrollably at Honolulu airport as we parted a week later. I was heading back to Britain and he was catching the next flight back to the Big Island and I was afraid that the dream would dissolve. But less than ten days later, having shared several astonishingly beautiful emails and phone calls, David arrived in the UK on a one-way ticket. Our engagement was announced a week later when we exchanged rings on Valentine's night under a full moon. Three months to the day after we first met, we were married in Las Vegas.

This story should comfort anyone who finds the thought of discovering their Eternal Flame among the vast population of the planet somewhat daunting. The truth is that if you and your Eternal Flame are meant to be together, you'll be pulled together with a force that is greater than magnetism. Inexorably, your lives will come together, possibly in a way, as with Barbara, that you could never have imagined. In fact, the harder you try to 'make' it happen, the more difficult it can become. This is because we tend to work out in great detail how it might happen, or how we can force it to happen, so that when we're meant to take a particular path, we end up putting obstacles in our own way or going in the wrong direction. That's when celestial signposts – whether coincidences, visions or messages – can help. But they can only do so if we leave the 'how' and the 'when' to the universe to arrange and just focus on the culmination of the story.

Be led and follow where you are guided.

CHAPTER 7

Down-to-earth Strategies for Finding a Soul Mate

If you're having trouble finding any soul mates at all, and you feel pretty alone, there are some down-to-earth methods that really seem to help. This chapter outlines the different approaches using people's stories by way of illustration and, in the case of hypnotherapy, the help of an expert to explain how it works.

'What if it's me?'

If you can be totally honest with yourself and admit that there is a problem within your own psyche that's preventing you from meeting any kind of soul mate, you're halfway to finding a solution, because if the problem lies with you, you are the only person who can fix it. If you take steps to sort out your own issues, it's quite likely that you could change your whole life.

HYPNOTHERAPY

Jacqueline Kirtley, an expert who has helped me in the past, explains how hypnotherapy can help someone with this issue:

There can be lots of reasons why we find close emotional relationships difficult. The kind of experiences and role models we have had as children will have moulded the way in which we respond to others now. The kind of person we are plays a part, as do our previous relationships. So how can we make a fully informed choice when we don't have all the information or we have the wrong information about how to have a mutually rewarding relationship that complements our lives?

Luckily, the emotional and behavioural patterns we develop in life are not set in stone. We develop them because they help us to deal with certain things in our experience, and they do tend to become habitual – for example, going from one abusive relationship to another. It is perfectly possible, however, to shed a pattern which is no longer useful and to develop new ones more suited to what we need in life now. The quickest and most effective way to do this is through hypnotherapy, which can help you to deal with the psychological and emotional issues that can arise in any relationship.

The thing that most people don't realise about hypnosis is that it is backed by a huge amount of scientific research. There's no magic or trickery; it's a process or state which has been researched by many people over an extended period of time. Relationship skills can be learned and it helps to talk to a trained professional who can teach you effective techniques to relax and be calm around others which can be a significant and positive benefit when trying to choose the right partner.

Hypnotherapy can help you to develop greater self-belief and positive thinking, leading to a new confidence in yourself and your ability to create successful relationships. It can help you to re-experience past memories and negative relationships in a more positive way and to gain new perspectives, neutralising feelings of anger and fear from the past so that they don't interfere in the present, therefore increasing your feelings of security and boosting your self-confidence so that you can make constructive and not destructive decisions about future partnerships.

Successful, healthy relationships are essential for fulfilling, stress-free lives. We have the power to make choices and we are in control. Hypnotherapy can provide a safe place to explore and change the negative aspects in our lives and relationships and allow us to make more positive and informed choices about our partners which, in turn, will benefit all areas of our lives.

What if there are no eligible partners in your area/social group?

It's not always easy to meet new people, especially if you live out in the countryside where the population is small, but there are some avenues open to everyone.

DATING AGENCIES AND CHAT ROOMS

Whereas long ago, people lived in tribes, worshipped in tribes and nurtured extended families, today many people live alone, feeling abandoned by the human race, their souls wilting. Today, families fragment, drift apart and live separate lives. It's all too easy to be alone and cut off, and it's incredibly hard for some people to develop any kind of social network, let alone meet that special someone.

So I do believe that organised dating agencies and internet 'chat rooms' have a role to play in bringing people who otherwise wouldn't have met, together. To make things safer, I'd suggest that you look at some of the 'spiritual dating sites' – the fact that you're reading this book means you are a spiritual person, so you're more likely to meet the right sort of people there. As always though, do be careful and when you meet someone for the first time make sure it's in a public place until you have had enough time to see into their soul.

Fay's story is a beautiful example of how love and, in this case, synchronicity, will find a way.

Fay's story

After my second marriage ended, I was figuring out what single people do, but not actively looking for a new partner. As far as I was concerned, it was just me and my son versus the world! I decided to go on Zoosk (an online forum for meeting people), merely to be nosy, when my ex-husband texted me asking why I was on it. He'd found me because I had come up as a match with him!

After going through many ifs and nos and maybes, I came

across Ian, my partner of two and a half years. Although I couldn't put my finger on just what it was about him (apart from his love of life and the fact that we could have a good laugh together) — something just felt right. Then we discovered we lived only five minutes away from each other and wondered how many times our paths must have crossed without us knowing!

Anyway, I've never looked back since, just forward.

The two stories that follow bring the saying 'love will find a way' to mind. I think this is perfectly true, but sometimes it does need a little help and determination.

Wendy's story

I met Scott nine years ago, via a chat room on the internet. I was really down, having had a breakdown while teaching. One evening, I was feeling particularly low and just needed someone to talk to. I'd never been on a chat room before, but felt maybe I could talk to someone without knowing them or ever meeting them. I observed for a while, then took the plunge. I got talking to a guy who seemed really sensitive. We chatted for hours and although I didn't say anything about my breakdown, I did tell him I was feeling low. We just seemed to click, and before I knew it five hours had gone by. I actually found myself laughing and felt so calm and happy.

There was something really kind about this man, but I was still really unsure as I had heard so many bad stories of women meeting murderers online. So I didn't tell him my real name or where I came from.

We kept arranging to meet online in the chat room and often sat up all night chatting. I opened up about my depression, and he seemed so understanding. All the while, I kept my guard up, just in case. We talked every night for a month and I found I was starting to fall for him in a big way. He said he felt the same way about me, and we decided at this point to swap mobile numbers. (I knew I could easily change my number if he did turn out to be dodgy.) After another couple of weeks, we arranged to meet up.

When we met face to face for the first time, it just felt so right. It really was just like coming home to a comfortable pair of slippers. I knew there and then that this was the man I was going to marry. It was as if we'd known each other all our lives, even though it had only been a total of seven weeks.

After that we met up every week, even though it meant travelling a 350-mile round trip. We spoke every day and just fell more and more in love. After a year, the travelling became too much and Scott decided he was going to move up to live with me. It was the best thing he's ever done.

When he moved up, I found a reading that I'd had done five years earlier telling me I was going to meet my soul mate. To be honest, I'd always thought I'd spend my life alone, but had thanked spirit for their message anyway. The reading had also told me that he would be in uniform and have a little boy to whom he was a father figure and that once we'd met he would never want to let me go. I smiled as I read all this. Scott was in the Army Cadets and had hoped to join the Army, but this dream would never be realised as he had bad hips. What's more, he has a nephew to whom he is a father figure. And the day he moved in,

Scott said to me: 'I knew the day I met you, that I never wanted to let you go!'

We've been together nine years now and will be celebrating our fifth wedding anniversary later this year. He's nursed me through some really difficult times and has stuck by me throughout. Not only is Scott my husband, he's my best friend and my soul mate too. I know we'll be together for ever.

Lisa's story

George and I met online. He had posted a profile at Salon.com and mine was buried in the Onion Online Personals! Little did we know that the two sites shared information. When we met for our first date at Casa del Mar and he said something about Salon, I thought: 'Oh no, I am having drinks with the wrong guy!' I couldn't believe we'd met through different websites.

In fact, we might have met much sooner, as George had emailed me the previous October, but I hadn't written back. I'd had several first dates, but no follow-ups and was beginning to feel quite bitter about online dating. Luckily though, George wrote to me again in January when I was feeling a little more positive, having been persuaded by a friend to try a new site. He was my first date after I posted on the Onion Personals. I was his third.

Our initial date lasted from four-thirty p.m. until almost nine. George later told me he almost hadn't shown up that night, thinking it would never go anywhere. But thank goodness he did turn up and with photos of a trip to Indonesia – the place in the world I most wanted to go to. He also shared photos from his time in the Peace Corps in

Paraguay. (George was surprised that I didn't bring my own photos.) I felt it was really sweet and showed a great side of him. My favourite recollection is of when he walked me to my car, kissed me and asked for a second date!

After dating for several months we travelled to Fiji and Vanuatu together. I had my first bucket-bath in a village where we stayed on the island of Vanuatu; we met the local Peace Corps worker in this one-generator village. It was a real window into George's life – so different from mine working on a cruise ship.

I can't believe I almost missed out on him by not writing back the first time. He wanted a partner who loved international travel and he says when he saw my profile, he just knew I was the one. And I managed to capture his interest by talking about the Shwedagon Pagoda. We have had to work on our travel styles as when we started we had such different ideas of the definition of great travel, but after tears, discussion and me learning to always carry my own toilet paper, it's worked out!

We got married nearly three years to the day after our first date and the wedding was at the hotel where we first met! I feel so fortunate that George found me online! He is my happily ever after.

PEN FRIENDS/PALS

If you are too shy to meet others face to face, but do not have internet access, becoming pen friends offers an opportunity to get to know someone first on an intellectual, rather than physical level. This can be a less intimidating way of meeting someone and can just as easily lead to a soul-mate relationship.

There are many lonely people in the world and there's nothing to say that your soul mate isn't out there hoping to find you. They are probably just as scared and alone as you are, and waiting for you to get in touch. One way is to start writing to soldiers. There are many men and women in the services and in action who have no family and no girlfriend or boyfriend. You never know where your support might lead, and the fact that they are in the military and therefore very accountable will help keep you safe.

Another way to do this is to write to prisoners. This might sound a bit risky and you'd have to be very careful indeed to be sure that you're strong enough to handle this kind of person. (Earlier in the book I gave an example of someone who did this successfully – see pp. 106–108). Who knows you might be their ticket to a new life and they might be yours?

Writing letters can also be a way to develop a relationship when the two of you have to live apart for a time. There are some avenues you might choose to explore in the Resources section – see p. 195.

♡♡ Michelle's story

I met and married my husband at a tender age and by the age of twenty-four I had four wonderful sons. However, the strain of four young children, a family-run business and the usual finance and day-to-day struggles took their toll on the marriage. I was a talker, a deep thinker and my husband was not; it no longer supported me, or his 'needs'. I had, in short, lost who I was.

Meanwhile, the work load was growing at his business, and as the children started school I began to work with him.

We found we needed another worker, so a young man joined the team. As the two 'unqualified' members, he and I were often set to work on mundane jobs together.

One day I had a phone call from this young man's mum, Deanna. We talked for an hour that first time and by the end of the conversation, I knew I had found a friend for life! Through Deanna and her son, I was being given a chance to be me. I was being heard as an individual, and the spark of 'me' was relit. This had the knock-on effect of making me recognise my need to renew my own desires, on my own terms and in my own time. The long and short of it was that the marriage was over.

I spent a whole tearful day putting my emotions and feelings on to paper, so as to get the whole of the matter across to my husband. Later, we held each other and cried together, as I told him that although I still loved him, I no longer saw our marriage working.

My husband gave me my amazing sons and our time together taught me many lessons: hardships, joys, perseverance, putting others first and, eventually, how to find myself once more, as the adult I now was. I moved out with the boys.

Meanwhile, Deanna moved abroad with her Forces husband and we continued to correspond. I heard that she had to have surgery, and I offered to take six weeks out and stay with her during her recovery. As a treat to me for helping out, she took me to her friend's house for a manicure and the three of us sat chatting over coffee. After a long conversation her friend said to me, 'You're perfect for my husband's friend Jon.' 'Oh, no!' I replied, 'I'm done with men!'

But a few days later we were invited to her friend's again for a coffee and so back we went. To my surprise, not only was the friend's husband at home, but there was also another man sitting at the table. The girls talked, the husband joined in a little, but the other man sat quietly for the most part. Just as we were about to leave, the friend mentioned that this man, Jon, was about to go on tour to Iraq for six months. Deanna jumped up with pen and paper asking for his contact details. 'Michelle loves to write letters,' she told him. All I could do was smile at this poor man's look of surprise. But I began a correspondence that very afternoon, thinking that if I wrote a 'bluey' (a special air-mail letter for the Forces) straight away, it would be in the post and arrive about the same time as he did. I saw him briefly a couple days later, just before my return to England, at which point I told him I'd already posted four blueys. He seemed surprised again, but happy that he'd have something waiting for him.

I've always been one to see signs around me – our fathers had the same Christian names, our parents' addresses were uncannily alike (Willoughby Avenue and Willow Avenue) my lucky numbers are seven and seventeen and Jon's Battery was seventeen. I was intrigued, and if my angels were trying to tell me something, I was listening!

I can't tell you how excited I was the day the postman handed me my first bluey! I was so nervous and my heart was fluttering. I just had a feeling that this was a big thing. In no time at all we'd exchanged all the basic information about ourselves with each other, then gone on to our likes and dislikes, our hopes and dreams and, by the time he returned, we both knew we'd found someone special.

I invited him to stay for a week during his annual leave and he agreed. He arrived on the Friday, we chatted, went for coffee and a walk along the quayside, and collected the boys from school. We spent a wonderful evening together and without the need for words, we were an item. Before his visit was over, it was decided that I would move abroad to be with him and only a few months later that's exactly what I had done. We married the following July, and that was eight years ago.

I remember that once on a visit to my auntie when I was younger I told her I thought I'd marry a soldier. Little did I know that it would take a strange sequence of events, some special people and a trip abroad to find him! I believe Jon is my soul mate, but I recognise also that my first husband, my sons, Deanna and her son are all part of my soul group also.

Getting out there

What if you never see anyone and long just to be among others? It's hard to go out and find people, especially if you're shy, and even more so if you've just come out of a bad relationship and are looking for someone special who won't hurt you again.

Try taking part in events and joining clubs where you don't immediately put pressure on yourself to communicate with others. Sport is one way to do this, especially those sports that don't require you to have a partner or someone to play against initially (swimming, golf, archery, clay-pigeon shooting, walking, horse-riding, etc.). Arts and craft groups can also be a good place to meet like-minded people. Even deep in the countryside there are craft groups where you can learn skills as diverse as hedge-laying and basketry. Being with people with shared interests will help you gradually to gain (or regain) your confidence and, eventually, to talk to them.

If you're alone and want to find people you can talk to, another good way to do this is via groups that provide surrogate 'grandchildren' for lonely older people or 'big brothers' for your own children. You never know what these social groupings may lead to, or who you could end up meeting (see Resources, p. 195).

Joanne's story

I met my soul mate on a golf course. I'd been playing for a few weeks alone, when I caught up with this chap who was more useless than me! He disarmed me with his humble nature because he didn't take the mickey out of women golfers as I'd expected. We ended up finishing the course together, we had a drink in the clubhouse and now I hope and am sure that we're going to finish up our life course together too.

What if you're not ready/in too much pain?

Sometimes we're so destroyed by a failed relationship or unrequited love that we cease to be able to function, let alone get 'back on the horse'. If you've been badly hurt to the point where you just can't bring yourself to think about another relationship, you need to do some inner healing before you even try.

CLOSE YOUR EYES AND EMBRACE IT

Here's a simple strategy to help you embrace and then let go of your pain so you can change the way you're thinking and feeling:

- Sit somewhere quietly and close your eyes.

- Now, focus on the pain. Let your emotions swamp and overwhelm you for a moment. It might seem cruel, but by focusing on the pain you'll find that you can sense it strongly in one particular part of your body. It may be your 'heart', but that's not always the case; it can also be your stomach or your head or just deep inside your abdomen.

- Once you've identified the part of your body where the pain feels strongest, concentrate on healing it in a practical way that makes sense to you, especially to your logical left brain (see p. 85). Over the next few days and weeks focus on healthy eating and lifestyle, especially things that will aid the part of your body that's internalising the pain. For instance, if it's your heart that feels it, then eat less sugar (which doctors now recommend over avoiding fats) and take exercise designed to strengthen the heart. If it's your stomach or digestive system, then cut out dairy foods that can cause blockages in those areas and take exercise to help build power in those abdominal muscles. Nurture yourself in this way and soon you'll find the pain easing.

- Once you reach a point where you're feeling less raw and a little bit stronger, just close your eyes again and do what I call, 'cutting the cord': picture your pain as a red balloon, tethered to the part of your body that aches. Now see yourself cutting that cord. Watch the balloon float up higher and higher, getting smaller and smaller until it vanishes altogether. If you practise this several times you will start to feel better!

Sally's story

I thought I was never going to get over the pain when Sam dropped me. We'd been married for five years and I honestly thought he loved me as much as I loved him. Then one day he just sat me down, told me it was over, packed his bags and was gone, out of my life – all within an hour. I sat there in disbelief, expecting him to walk back in and admit he was wrong.

When I tried to get my life back on track I just couldn't be bothered, but eventually I tried what Jenny suggested. The pain was in my heart and I managed to galvanise myself into nurturing that part of my body. It helped, I think, because it gave me something to focus on. Instead of continuing to try and suppress the pain, I felt I was doing something about it. It made me feel less like a victim and not so hopeless and helpless.

After a while I was able to do the 'cord cutting'. The first few times I resisted, feeling that by letting go I was somehow betraying my love, but then Jenny explained that I wasn't letting go of the love at all, only the pain, and so I was able to do it.

Six months later I met Simon at a friend's daughter's birthday party. He's a single dad, and had trouble finding someone to take on both him and two-year-old Joshua. That someone is me.

Getting through the holiday season

Holidays are a particularly difficult time for those who feel alone as they watch lit rooms through frosty windows and wonder why they're always on the outside looking in. If money is short the problem is exacerbated as they can't even go and join in a party with acquaintances at the local pub if they can't afford to buy a round of drinks.

PLACES WHERE YOU CAN BE AMONG PEOPLE

Luckily, at this time of year almost anyone can get a job in one of the major department stores as they're always looking for extra staff over the big buying seasons and this can be a good way to get yourself out and around other people. If you're too shy to deal with people on the shop floor, there's often work 'backstage' in the warehouse areas, picking goods to be sent to the shop floor. Many small independent shops also welcome the extra help at Christmas time and it could lead to something permanent.

If your priority is finding someone to talk to as opposed to earning money, charity/thrift stores might not be able to pay you, but they will make you feel welcome. You could also help out at a soup kitchen. You'll gradually strike up friendships with the other volunteers and may get invited to functions – and who knows who you might meet there.

Joining a local church is another way to avoid being alone. You'll be surprised at how quickly the place can become somewhere you feel you belong.

Be willing to be led because your soul mate is out there somewhere.

Mel's story

I've always been a loser, or that's how I saw myself. I lived in a small town and I was gay. I'd proudly 'come out' to my parents, who were surprisingly supportive as they waited for me to bring home this 'man of my dreams'. But after the initial euphoria of becoming myself I found the reality was harsh. As far as I knew there were no other gay men in town; not that I could find, anyway. It had been bad enough being rejected by girls, but to come on to a man, and then have him laugh at me and say he was straight or didn't fancy me or maybe even hit me? I could not do it.

I'd also been out of work, so that didn't help either. I had no money to go anywhere and no one to talk to. I got very low, skulking at home. Mum and Dad who had obviously been a little shocked initially and probably dreaded having to accept a male partner, now started to worry that they were never even going to get the chance.

Christmas was coming and although I had my parents, I needed some friends of my own. I finally got a job at Littlewoods, in the warehouse, selecting goods for people to buy from the catalogues. I met Tommy. He wasn't gay, but he knew right away that I was, and he didn't mind. We became pals and he invited me out for a drink (strictly as friends – he made that clear). But to my amazement he took me to a gay bar. I didn't even know there was such a thing!

I still haven't found my life partner, but that night changed my life and I'm sure I soon will.

Vivien's story is another example of how the workplace can bring soul mates into contact with each other. It's no surprise really because there are few other situations where so many different people can be put into each other's paths. I wonder if this union is a temporary one as they are not always comfortable with each other, and it's possible they're more likely to be Twin/Teacher soul mates, rather than Eternal Flames, but time will tell.

♡♡ Vivien's story

Since my spiritual life began blooming, I've become keenly aware that my personal life is guided, just as the rest of my path has been.

I've encountered many soul mates on my path, of all kinds. However, the most powerful one arrived, suddenly and unexpectedly, last October. We 'found' each other as he walked into my office at work to submit his PhD thesis, the culmination of seven years' work. I too was at the end of a massive cycle, although at the time I was unaware. Before I even saw him, I felt his energy come into the room. We exchanged looks on more than one occasion and I found myself thinking about him that evening, sensing that something had occurred – energetically at least.

I'd just moved to this office, and many people come in who I don't know. My colleague knew this man well though, and before I knew it, she was trying to get us together. She sensed something herself. The meeting came at a time when we were both at the end of a cycle, and in the months that followed we were adjusting to a massive energy implosion – in my case, a huge spiritual transition and, in his, a time of adjusting to his own issues.

This union has a very special spiritual link and I believe issues that are being worked through currently are from the past, but it is that link that is very strong. My spiritual growth has bloomed, with clairaudience (the gift of being able hear spirits) and incredible dreams, some of them related to this relationship. A bond has developed and we are mirrors to each other. At times it is uncomfortable, and there was a two-week period when harsh words were exchanged and I believed it was over. But his energy had never gone, as I found out when he 'returned'.

I'm strongly guided in my actions with this relationship and behave in a way that is unfamiliar to me, but I try to trust it. The return was only three weeks ago and things are blooming again. An inexplicable connection has been made, along with mutual learning, growth through gentle friendship, and with each one teaching the other so much. Never have I experienced such a meeting of minds and spirit as I have with him, and such incredible similarities. He has a wonderful mind and is very spiritually aware and there's no way this would have even happened without spirit guidance, as we don't even live in the same place. I also see why I've had to experience the difficult soul mates I have had in order to prepare me for this. All is clear now. It certainly feels like this is a soul who's here to stay, but we never know.

I look forward to seeing how it unfolds . . .

I know, from all the letters I receive, how easy it is for people to feel like giving up. But what does this achieve? If you are in this situation, ask yourself if you really have tried everything. And, if you have honestly done so, then perhaps you should consider that you need to stop trying – completely stop trying and concentrate on yourself. I say this because it may well be that although you do have a perfect soul mate out there, you won't become a perfect match until you've changed the circumstances of your own life. Doing this for yourself may be something you absolutely need to do in this lifetime, and once you do, just like the cogs in a machine, everything will start to click into place.

Nothing puts off potential partners and friends more than someone who comes across as needy and desperate, so ask yourself if you fall into this category. But don't worry if you think you do – the remedy is simple: just open your heart to trusting the universe and let your obsession float away from your mind. Trust that you deserve and will find what you're looking for. It can be a great release to do this, as you absolve yourself of responsibility and relieve the pressure you have been piling on yourself.

CHAPTER 8

Mystical Means for Finding Your Soul Mate

It has to be said that soul mates are destined to find each other, and therefore, most often, they do so naturally. But sometimes we hold up the process by thinking we know best and, perhaps, pushing in the wrong direction. There are many mystical ways purported to help you find your soul mate, but do any of them work? Surprisingly, you might think, some of them do and the methods described in this chapter can certainly help to direct events more efficiently.

Aura

Every little thought we have travels through the neurons in our brain via electrical activity and, like any other electrical device, we humans create an energy field around ourselves. This is an aura. Couple that with the fact that we are also spiritual creatures with souls, and you can see why our auras are much more complex, effective and informative that those of your vacuum cleaner or washing machine. Unlike machines, our auras change colour and vibrancy, depending on our physical and spiritual wellbeing and, to a large extent, our personality traits.

Our auras emanate from our chakras. Chakra means 'wheel' in Sanskrit, and the body has several spinning energy centres that resemble spinning wheels. These chakras regulate the flow of energy through our spiritual system. There are seven chakras, the crown, brow (or third eye), throat, heart, solar plexus, centre and root, all creating colours in our energy fields.

If you've ever met somebody new and immediately felt like backing away from them, it could well be that your auras are not compatible; similarly, instant attraction and a feeling of comfort when someone comes into your personal space, means that your auras are in balance with each other.

USING AURAS

To use auras to select a mate, you have to learn to see and interpret them:

- Sit relaxed in a chair next to a plain and preferably light-coloured wall.

- Raise one hand level with your eyes, with the fingers splayed.

- Stare at your fingertips, but let your eyes go 'soft' so that they start to concentrate on the air just above them. With a little patience you will start to see a fuzzy outline around the tips of your fingers, almost like a double image or the air disturbance seen around a fast-moving vehicle or a mirage in the desert. Once you can see this, move your hand slowly from side to side, and you'll see that the image follows them. Now you should be able to see that the outline goes down between your fingers too. The harder and longer you stare the clearer this aura will become. After a while you'll notice that the outline flares at the top, and starts to look more like tendrils of smoke than an outline with a sharp edge.

• Now place your hands, palms together, in front of you. Focus on the aura between them and then slowly draw them apart. As your hands move further apart, the two auras of your hands will separate.

Once you've done this you'll probably wonder how you never saw auras before, and if you try, you'll be able to see them around everything – even trees and rocks.

THE COLOURS OF LOVE

The next thing you need to learn is to start seeing colours. This takes nothing more than practice, practice and practice.

Start by getting some friends to act as guinea pigs for you – I've yet to meet anyone who isn't immediately interested and willing to help when you ask, 'Can I look at your aura?' Colours will come gradually, starting with one or two, until you can build the whole shape of the person in wavy blocks of colour. And don't forget, with auras people have no choice but to show their true colours.

Before you start using your new-found skill, you need to know what the colours actually mean:

- **Indigo:** a healer who can soothe your troubled soul, but might be bland and dull
- **Black:** a troubled soul themselves, who could be very needy and demanding
- **Pastel blue:** will endorse your emotions and be a tender and considerate lover; can be lacking in ambition
- **Sky blue:** a natural person who cares for the world, but might not have enough time to give you attention
- **Petrol blue:** intuitive – and will always know what you are thinking, which means they will know if you're lying
- **Royal blue:** a decisive person who knows where they're going (be careful you don't get flattened along the way)
- **Turquoise:** a sea lover, so not for someone who wants a stay-at-home partner, but very romantic
- **Dark blue:** steady and safe; not adventurous
- **Mauve/blue:** has psychic ability, so there will be no hiding your innermost thoughts and desires
- **Orange:** strong and courageous; liable to succeed where others fail (not a pipe-and-slippers person)
- **Toffee:** a career chaser; can be ruthless, but will be a good provider
- **Beige:** washed out and depleted through problems experienced, but 'colour' and vibrancy are showing signs of returning
- **Chocolate brown:** an environmentalist, who will spend most of their time saving whales, so if you are 'high maintenance' you might not be well-suited
- **Rust:** a hard worker/provider – can be a bit overly humble and can turn into a doormat
- **Terracotta:** rebel with or without a cause – you say black,

they'll say white, but they'll be fun with never a dull
moment

- **Gold:** sincere and honest; highly evolved spiritually, but
  maybe a little staid
- **Pale green:** spiritually advanced, but still a learner, so apt to
  be confused and require long heart-to-heart discussions
- **Lemon yellow:** a liar – liable to be unfaithful
- **Mid-green:** able to heal you and willing to do so, no matter
  how many times you need it, but can be boring if you're a
  party animal
- **Bright grass green:** friendly, gregarious – this means life
  and soul of the party, but not so good one to one
- **Dark green:** can be mean, but thrifty, which is useful if you
  are always spending out of control
- **Grey:** feels trapped and depressed and may pull you down
- **Peach:** a good talker/listener, but this means all the time –
  even when your favourite soap is on
- **Pale pink:** looking for true love, but inclined to soppy
  behaviour, so if being showered with gifts in public might
  be an embarrassment, probably not one for you
- **Bright pink:** happy in driving their career forward, but will
  insist that you need to be that way too, so might come
  across as a little pushy, if you're not ambitious
- **Violet:** has usually had a profound, life-changing
  experience which has balanced and humbled them – a good
  mate, but not feisty in a fight
- **Magenta:** entrepreneur, with fingers in every pie; can have
  criminal tendencies if not controlled
- **Bright red:** creative, but self-opinionated
- **Rusty red:** argumentative and not willing to listen, but if
  they're on your side in an argument, they will never quit

- **Silver:** well connected to their angels, but a tendency to spend long hours in meditation
- **Pearly:** medium abilities, so inclined to bring spooky goings-on into your home
- **Bright yellow:** a dreamer – sweet, gentle and harmless, but not especially productive
- **Pale primrose yellow:** caring, empathetic and compassionate; this does mean that if you're on your way to a party, they will insist on stopping for the injured toad and taking it to a rescue centre, regardless of whether you are wearing an Armani dress

Once you have learned to see and interpret the colours, they can be used in two ways:

1. You can read your own colours and go for someone with similar ones to yours. This will give you a partner with similar ideas and plans and if you are both on the same level spiritually, the two of you will rarely disagree. But like to like doesn't always work; for instance, if both of you have the colour of rusty red, you will quarrel endlessly and never make up. Don't choose someone who is a depressive (grey) if you are too, as each of you could be too weak to help the other recover.

2. Go for colours that complement yours and fill in the gaps in your persona. For instance, if you are often dreaming, but not achieving much (bright yellow), go for a partner whose aura is orange (liable to succeed) or magenta (an entrepreneur) who might be able to help make your dreams come true!

Of course, you may well see several bright colours in one person. If that's the case, then for the purposes of this exercise – i.e. finding your soul mate – you should concentrate on the heart area and the colour around it. This is the area that deals with perceptions and feelings regarding other people, so this will interest you most when looking for someone to love you.

If you have an aura photograph taken or have your aura read by a psychic, you can use your predominant or heart colour to match yourself up with the most compatible colour for you. Here are some examples of complementary pairings:

- **Orange and beige:** a combination that will bring the power and determination of orange to the beige, which needs strong support and a bit of a push
- **Rust and dark blue:** the conscientious rust brings security and stability to the dark blue, which needs a settled life without dramas
- **Terracotta and dark green:** the argumentative side of terracotta can be curbed by the practical dark green, perhaps channelling their joint energy more efficiently
- **Gold and mauve:** the sincerity of gold makes the sensitive mauve feel protected and accepted, and their innermost dreams respected without ridicule
- **Mid-green and grey:** the mid-green healer will just keep on giving, no matter how much support the wistful grey seems to need, and will enjoy doing so
- **Peach and pink:** very loving colours with plenty of romantic gestures from both; this combination will enjoy hours of heartfelt discussions and emotional support from each other

- **Bright pink and magenta:** both career colours, they will inspire each other's ambitions and support left-field ideas and creative bombshells without flinching
- **Rusty red and violet:** the rusty red will always be on the side of the downtrodden and humble violet, fighting if necessary to defend them, while faithful and true, the violet will calm the rusty red
- **Silver and pale green:** a good angel communicator, the advanced silver will give the pale green spiritual insight and enhance their desired soul development with patience and courage
- **Pearly and pale primrose yellow:** prone to seeing spirits, pearly colours will complement the caring, empathetic and compassionate primrose
- **Indigo and black:** the indigo healer will support the troubled black, bringing understanding to this needy character, while the black will allow the indigo to utilise their need to rescue, by accepting help
- **Pastel blue and toffee:** not a career chaser, the laid-back pastel blue will be happy to support the toffee, who is quite the reverse, and will need an understanding partner, for whom they will provide in abundance
- **Sky blue and royal blue:** a lover of the planet, the sky-blue dreamer needs the drive and ambition of a royal blue, who'll run roughshod over the opposition
- **Petrol blue and bright yellow:** the petrol blue colour is honest and compassionate, so they'll keep the bright yellow's feet on the ground, while allowing them freedom to dream
- **Turquoise and chocolate brown:** the oceanic, globe-trotting turquoise will team up beautifully with the independent

environmentalist that is the chocolate brown, and together they will save the planet

- **Bright grass green and red:** the bright green is one of the few colours that can tame the opinionated red, and bring balance to an otherwise volatile life; bright green loves a challenge which red will provide

Note: one colour to avoid, and certainly to change if you have it is the pale lemon aura. This person can be deceitful and may even lie to themselves.

♡♡ Jane's story

I tended always to wear quiet, even dull colours, and was only attracting men wearing the same sort of colours. By the age of thirty-two, I still hadn't had a meaningful relationship, let alone found a soul mate. All my potential partners were 'drips' and we soon drifted apart. After learning about auras and gradually being able to see them for myself, I soon realised that what I needed was to brighten my own, which can be done by wearing different colours. I started with pastels, which weren't too scary, and I found I soon started to attract a different sort of date. By the time I'd graduated in confidence to wearing red, I met Gary. He was a real go-getter, and in earlier days I would have run a mile. But that was ten years ago, and now Gary and I are celebrating our eighth wedding anniversary. We couldn't be happier.

Spells

Do spells work? Can you possibly attract the right soul mate using magic? Is it right to 'force' someone – in a sense – to love you? The truth is that it simply isn't possible to force someone to love someone else. What this spell and others like it might achieve, however, is to bring your own and your soul mate's energy to life in a way that helps you to connect. Let me know how you get on!

- Fill a pretty bowl with some filtered or purified water (good mineral water will work).
- Pick two blossoms from the garden, or dried leaves if there are no flowers.
- Hold each in turn in your cupped hands and name one with your name and the other with the name of your soul mate.
- Place them carefully on to the surface of the water, and as they float and draw together (as they will), say: 'This is the way our paths will cross, whether we live parted by seas or skies or mountains, we will be pulled together by forces we are unable to resist.

It's important that once you've done this you hand your request over to the universe and accept 'heaven's timescale'. In other words: stop pushing. Keep the flowers or leaves floating in the water as long as they're alive. When they have shrivelled, it will be time for your dreams to start to come true.

♡♡ Peggy's story

I had all but given up hope of my soul mate taking any notice of me, when I stumbled across a spell using a white flower. I think I was led to it. It was in an old book in the library and the book opened on this page, as if by magic. The spell involved pinning six white flowers into my hair and leaving them there for twenty-four hours. Then I had to light a candle and burn them in the flame, while saying the name of the man I love. Six days later he asked me out, and we've now been together for six months. I think we might end up with six children!

Plants

The power of flowers and plants to affect us – both emotionally, with their beauty and scent and through their medicinal properties – is well documented, but they can also affect the path of love. Surrounding yourself with the right blossom's perfume can make you attractive to the right person. In her book *The Scent of Desire* Rachel Herz shows that smell has a much greater part to play in sexual attraction than may previously have been understood.

Here are some flowers that might help you in your quest:

- Roses, especially red ones, are said to encourage a proposal of marriage.
- Two wands of hazel bound together are said to be able to heal an argument.
- Poppy seeds when placed in a pillow case are said to bring sweet dreams of you to the person who sleeps on it.

- Lavender is said to heal the soul and purge the pain of past betrayals, so opening your heart to new love.
- Once you have your soul mate with you, a pot of cowslips by your front door is said to keep the unwelcome from interfering or trying to come between you.

♡ Janice's story

My girlfriend Louise and I had been going out for several years and moved in together, but I wanted more commitment in our relationship, something public, a declaration. I was too scared to ask her to 'marry' me though in case she laughed or thought it was silly. So after reading about the power of flowers I chose the rose and I filled our flat with petals, all creating a path to the bedroom, where I had champagne on ice. I can't honestly say whether the petals helped, but they certainly didn't hinder, because she did ask me, that very same night, and we're having a civil ceremony in two weeks' time!

Numerology

The science of numbers has been used for hundreds of years. Numerology is very simple to work with and can be a valuable tool to help you in your quest to find your one Eternal Flame.

To make love a reality instead of just dreaming about it, find your inner-wisdom number by using your name and the table below. Each letter has a numerical value as follows:

1	2	3	4	5	6	7	8	9
A	B	C	D	E	F	G	H	I
J	K	L	M	N	O	P	Q	R
S	T	U	V	W	X	Y	Z	.

You reach your inner-wisdom number by adding together the numbers that correspond to the letters in your name, then reducing the final number down until you reach a single digit (so for a total of 37, you would add the 3 and 7 together to make 10, then 1 + 0 = 1). Once you have your inner-wisdom number you can find out what it signifies by looking at the list below. Recognising your character traits and the type of partner you need will give you a better chance of finding and building a good relationship, even if it is with a Twin Soul rather than an Eternal Flame.

- If you are a **1**, you are very strong and need a partner who is one of two extremes, either very strong also, or very malleable.
- A **2** is very honest and can't accept lies in any form, so you won't want a partner who plays games and you won't play them either. Openness and honour are the words of the day.
- A **3** loves to party and won't want the slippers by the TV for quite a few years, so you need an adventurous partner who doesn't mind spending money on a good time.
- As a **4,** you need to feel safe and secure. You're sensitive, so you'll want a stable partner, who understands your emotional needs. You'd be intimidated by film-star looks, so go for a gentle sense of humour and plenty of hugs.

- A **5** has great intelligence and a huge zest for life, so you need a partner who is equally smart and who'll stimulate you mentally. You'll never be happy with just good looks and neither will your ideal partner.

- If you are a **6**, you are quickly committed to a partner and want all the 'settling-down' trimmings, so you won't be happy with an adventurous traveller. You're a true romantic so you need a partner who appreciates hearts and roses.

- A **7** will never settle for second best, but would rather wait for perfection. You tend to over-analyse every word though, so you need someone who thinks before they speak and considers the reaction of every action they take.

- As an **8**, you are quite naturally very attractive to the opposite sex (and the same sex too). Because of this you'll be presented with a big field to play. You need a partner who will be somewhat independent though because you don't like clingy types.

- A **9** believes that marriage is to create a family and so you are likely to have children very young. You can be very emotional, so you need a mature partner who has good morals and a strong sense of right and wrong.

Ask your angels or God to help you

Prayer is meditation by another name. Sitting quietly and closing off your mind, while asking whatever power you believe in to listen to your pleas is universal. It doesn't require affiliation to a particular religious group, just a heartfelt and genuine need to be heard.

Destiny is a strange thing. To some extent, I believe we all have a path to walk and a destination to reach, but I also believe we have free will and, therefore, an ability to change the course of that path. If we go off our path, sometimes we have to ask for some help to get back on to it and back to the place where we need to be to connect with our soul mates.

Those who have read my other books will know how much faith I have in angels and their ability to help us, so I'm very happy to include Jennifer's story as it shows that angels will even help us find our soul mate.

Jennifer's story

I think it's important to leave room for the universe to surprise us and I'm learning why now. I believe we are sent a mate to help us trigger and heal our deepest heartbreaks, if we're up to doing the work.

I met my soul mate on a business trip to Berlin to celebrate the five-year anniversary of the company I was working for at the time. After the big celebration dinner, some co-workers and I decided to continue the party elsewhere. As we descended into the dark Berlin club, I noticed Tani instantly under the hot spotlights. His coffee-coloured hair, olive skin and striped sweater screamed European. He looked like something I'd ordered off the internet. Through intense brown eyes, his gaze held me hostage. I danced wildly and smiled to myself. As our group started heading home, I made my move. In broken German, Tani told me that he was from Albania and was an artist. He later showed me a watercolour work he'd done. As he led me to the dance floor, his leather jacket brushed my cheek. I felt like I was home. It was 23 January 2009.

We walked to the hotel – the Motel One. Later on awakening, Tani put my number into his phone. We grabbed dinner that night at a café. In the morning, I kissed him goodbye on the rainy street. I watched as he turned up his collar and walked away.

Back in New York, I texted Tani a few times, but then stopped. I went to a Valentine's Day retreat in the woods. Deep in meditation, I heard 'Tani, Tani' in my heart. I wrote to him and he replied, excited to hear from me.

I'd planned a spring trip to London to visit a girlfriend, but when I couldn't confirm it I Googled Berlin instead. I'd fallen in love with the city, its gorgeous graffiti and so much more. I booked the flight and told Tani I'd be there soon. Back at Motel One for a night, we moved to our holiday home the next day.

We settled into a groove of cafés, street photography and watching *The Wire*. I was hooked. At the airport once more I told him I'd be back by 1 May. Then I quit my job, sublet my apartment and packed my bags. On 28 April 2009, I took a cab to Tani's apartment. He'd bought adorable heart sheets for the bed we'd share there. I moved to a flat, but spent just one night there. Instead, it evolved into my 'office', where I wrote during the day. In June, Tani asked me to move in with him. Albanian hospitality at its best. I was thirty-eight and accustomed to much more autonomy, but I said yes and never looked back.

A statue of Archangel Michael stands vigil in Mitte. Passing it one day, I paused and heard the words, 'Marry this man'. I told Tani and he smiled. For a few days, we joked about it. But it didn't feel funny in my heart, nor in his. I explained how an American woman needed a ring, bended knees and a proper proposal for it to be 'official'. The next Sunday, we browsed an antique mall for rings. I stood outside afterwards and the tears began to fall. For two years, I'd been asking God for my soul mate. I'd made 'Dream Man' lists and updated them often for about two years, with all the qualities I wanted in a mate and how I would feel being with him. While Tani's not 100 per cent of the things I 'ordered', he fits! I'd made vision boards and MANifestation maps with hot dark-haired men. And there we were, in Berlin, shopping for rings!

Later that night, Tani knelt down, handed me a beautiful ring and asked me to marry him. Completely stunned, but unhesitating, I said, 'Yes!' He called his parents and I emailed mine.

On 3 July 2009, we were married at a small office in Dushk, Albania. Town workers were our witnesses; we grabbed an ice-cream cone afterwards. We celebrated with Tani's family that night. Ours was a simple feast of meat, salad, feta cheese, French fries and freshly baked bread. We were happy, in love, two peas in a married pod. And it all started one night in Berlin.

Crystals

Selecting the right crystals to find your soul mate can depend on what you feel might be holding you up in your search.

For example, red stones such as rubies and red garnets are all said to heighten passion, but of course, you first have to decide whether it's passion that's lacking in your life. So think about what you might like to change about yourself and start there.

If shyness is an issue and it stops you from having the confidence to admit to love, try carrying some malachite with you (whether a tumblestone or a piece of jewellery) and see what happens. Not only will it give you confidence, but it will also give you assertiveness without aggression as it balances your energy. It will also help you to offer fearless love, without constraint, so you won't miss an opportunity to pair up with your soul mate.

Rose quartz is the stone for self-love, so if you feel you're being held back because you don't think you're loveable or deserve love, this stone should help you dispel those feelings of inadequacy.

If you've been badly hurt in the past, then lavender jade, like its namesake plant will bring calmness and trust that new love will heal, rather than damage. It will help remove old thought patterns caused by distress in the past and also enable you to detach more easily from a clingy ex.

Once you think you've discovered the right person, a twin quartz crystal will help seal the deal. This is a pair of aligned crystals that have grown together and were – at least originally – attached along their length. These crystals will help you focus on the important parts of your relationship.

Once you and your soul mate are together and marriage or some sort of commitment is likely, you can also choose the stone in the ring you give each other with care. Diamonds are the obvious choice and do symbolise never-ending love and devotion, but emerald is another good one as it stands for fidelity and honesty. Opal, on the other hand, recognises the need for sustaining passion in a long-term relationship and the fiery kind will ensure your sparks continue to fly.

The bedroom is often the hub of any issues that could mar your happiness, so this is where I would suggest putting a crystal grid, which uses several crystals placed in a specific pattern. For the 'master' (or top) stone I have chosen turqurenite, which is actually a dyed form of howlite, the colour change slightly altering its properties towards encouraging passion. The centre stone should always be a clear quartz, as these are the most spiritual of all stones, and their purity signifies angelic energy. The other six stones I would recommend for this are black tourmaline (for understanding), howlite (to prevent insomnia), citrine (the 'cuddle stone', so that even when you're without your partner, you won't feel lonely), two more clear quartz stones (to make sure you are in tune together or apart, by mirroring each other) and selenite (so that shared journeys, whether through the paths of passion or sleep, are harmonious and filled with spiritual awareness).

Here are some other crystals you might find helpful:

- **Amazonite:** helps the mind remain calm during times of stress, enabling you to use your intuition while also being practical
- **Amber:** attracts happiness and happy people to you
- **Amethyst:** absorbs negativity; soothes night fears and panic attacks
- **Aventurine:** calms tempers and brings balance to a relationship
- **Azurite:** helps to dispel arguments caused by resentment
- **Blue lace agate:** allows self-expression without aggression
- **Blue topaz:** gives people the ability to communicate more fully
- **Carnelian:** assists in decision making, aiding choice in important issues

- **Celestite:** encourages peace and serenity
- **Chrysocolla:** brings harmony and peace to a damaged heart
- **Chrysoprase:** moving home puts a lot of stress on relationships; this will bring success to new enterprises
- **Citrine:** known as the 'cuddle stone', this will give you a feeling of having company even if you are lonely, and encourage a standoffish partner to be more tactile and to display affection
- **Garnet:** helps you to be persistent when striving to reach a goal, and brings clarity to what you think you want
- **Hematite:** gives self-esteem, while keeping your feet on the ground
- **Kyanite:** emotionally calming and strengthening
- **Labradorite/spectrolite:** helps you to 'see' more clearly
- **Lapis lazuli:** reveals inner truth and encourages meaningful communion
- **Moonstone:** restores emotional balance, especially to those who find expressing their emotions difficult
- **Peridot:** helps to disperse tension, especially when feelings have been hurt
- **Rhodonite:** enables patience and harmony, while giving you enough assertiveness to help you stand your ground
- **Rose quartz:** brings self-love, heals emotional wounds and helps to overcome grief of any kind
- **Sodalite:** brings clarity to the mind; stops oversensitivity
- **Sugilite:** brings out your own inner power and light for all to see
- **Smoky quartz:** washes away negative beliefs and emotions, including those brought about by hurtful pasts
- **Tiger's eye:** helps us make our dreams come true

- **Turquoise:** makes decisions clearer, as you see what you really need – as opposed to what you think you want
- **Turquenite:** brings passion and vitality

Cosmic ordering

What this means in its simplest form is writing down a list – just like a shopping list – of everything you'd want your soul mate to be. It originates from the belief that the universe acts as a kind of mirror, reflecting your belief back to you, sometimes as a physical manifestation. Once you've written the list, making it as detailed and as definitive as you possibly can, you can either just forget about it and leave the how and when up to the universe, or you can keep it by your bed and read it every day. Some people light a candle and burn their list in the flame, others bury it somewhere, in the moonlight. I'm not sure that the means of disposal makes any difference to the outcome, but I do know that making these lists (in all aspects of your life) *does* work, having done it myself many times.

Here's an interesting story involving cosmic ordering and balloons!

♡♡ Nicole's story

I met my partner in London on the same day that I sent a piece of paper with the qualities of my perfect partner written on it up in a helium balloon.

The first day we spoke was an interesting one for me, having done one of the silliest yet liberating things I have done in my adult life. As you might have gathered I am a bit of a cynic, yet underneath it all is a hopeful girl praying that all her jaded views of the world are false and that all her bad experiences have been a lie and not the true representation of the human spirit.

Some time ago when I was talking to a friend, she shared with me the concept of making 'a list' (cosmic ordering). It stems from the belief that what you put out in the universe as a thought or feeling will, if strong enough, come back to you. For example, if you believe and constantly say that you have bad luck and nothing works out for you, your mind will ensure that you never succeed – not for lack of opportunity, but for a lack of faith in yourself and your own possibilities.

So after a horrible break-up my friend had decided to write down what her ideal partner in life would be, as a message to the universe. She wrote down everything she could think of from brains to bone – all the things she would value in a man. After writing her list she met a man and after a fairly short courtship, he proposed. One day while spring cleaning, she stumbled across the list at the bottom of a pile of papers. Sure enough he met close to everything on that list. She believed he came into her life because she willed him to; she'd sent out a message and somehow the person who was right for her at that point in her life had answered.

I immediately dismissed this concept, giving her a million 'logical' explanations, but deep down, the hopeful girl in me was excited and almost giddy and I wanted to try it myself.

About two years ago, I broke off contact with a man who had been in my life since I was twenty – my first love. It was something that took a lot of strength, but I did it because I knew he wasn't what I wanted or needed to be happy. I began to think about what I did want and found myself writing 'my list'. I held on to the list, almost without even thinking about it, and not putting much faith into it because I knew I wasn't ready if HE showed up. I was emotionally a wreck, in a place of instability in my work life and I wanted to use my new freedom to have fun! A part of me also believed that I didn't have to rely on a piece of paper to ensure some level of happiness. I walked around with this list for over two years. It would drop out of notebooks or wallets every couple months, as if to ask: 'Nicole, are you ready yet?' I would shove it away promising it that soon I would be ready. I also romanticised how I would communicate that I was ready. My plan was to put my list in a helium balloon and let it go – almost like a priority message to the universe. (The silly, hopeful girl inside me came up with that idea.)

I decided to let go of my list a week after I'd stopped dealing with someone in London. It wasn't anything serious, but it was significant enough for me to come to the realisation that I was finally ready. I grabbed my list, bought a helium balloon from the local card shop and placed the list inside it. Then I went to a park, walked into the middle of a clearing and, with shaking hands, I let my dreams go. I started crying, just full of hope and fear. I couldn't believe how relieved I felt. Then suddenly, I was ecstatic – laughing and smiling to myself in the middle of the park with people looking at me as if I was insane. But I did it. Rational, cynical Nicole did it.

That night was the night we started emailing each other. I just logged on to my computer to see, and there was a smile from him. He had arrived in my life, just like that.

A few of my girlfriends have tried this and within months landed in serious relationships. Some lasted and some did not. My friend who introduced me to the concept ended up engaged to the man she met after writing her list. They moved to a different state, bought a home and started working in the same office. The relationship deteriorated and she revised her list, making tweaks and revisions to reflect things she discovered she needed in a partner. Shortly after the break-up she started dating a co-worker – someone she would not have met unless she'd moved to that state and got a job in that office. She is now married and has had a baby. She finally got it right.

WISH BOX

Cosmic ordering by any name can help in your quest to find a soul mate. In this case it's a wish box, which can be any container from a cardboard shoe box to an ornate jewellery box, but the more trouble you take over decorating it and making it entirely personal to you, the stronger and more connected to you it will be, and the more it will enable your mind and soul to be in tune with it, and open to messages that can lead you to where you need to go.

Fill the box with whatever reminds you of your soul mate and the life you might have with them: pictures of actual people who might resemble them, pictures of homes you might live in, children you might have or just beautiful things that create beautiful thoughts when you look at them. These boxes don't have any real magical properties, but a lot of people believe we can create our own reality, and a box like this attunes your subconscious to 'create' the right things.

♡♡ Doreen's story

I have a lovely jewel-encrusted box that someone gave me as a present, with a mirror in the lid. I have all the qualities that I'd like in my soul mate written on pieces of coloured card in there. When I wrote them out I imagined or visualised each quality in the man who would come into my life, then carefully placed them with love into the box. I take them out some nights when I get into bed and go over them one by one. This helps me not to feel lonely, as I still suffer from past hurts, which I hope to do more work on really soon. I have every belief that he's not too far away, and after many disastrous relationships – all lessons for me on my life's journey – I now see myself growing on into my autumn years with my Twin soul mate.

The internet

Crazy though it might seem, ancient mystical forces do sometimes use modern technology to get messages through to us, whether about soul mates or other subjects. The internet, otherwise known as the World Wide Web might just be the way to snare love. In the story that follows Eleanor hasn't found her soul mate yet, but I'm willing to bet that it won't be long before she's led right to him.

♡♡ Eleanor's story

I recently borrowed books from a friend of mine from the *Haunted Liverpool* series by Tom Slemen. There was a story I was particularly intrigued by called 'The Answer to Everything', which claimed that a man uncovered the code to answer everything using Pi. Anyway, there was said to be a website (http://pi.nersc.gov/) where you could type in your name and it would tell you the name of your future spouse.

I eagerly entered my name, but couldn't understand the codes, so I went to type in my sister's name, which is Sarah, but as I typed in the letter 'S', a drop-down opened with the words written: '*siempre ser tu mismo*'. I was absolutely sure this message was for me, though it had nothing to do with the purpose of the website. I translated it from Spanish to English; it meant 'Always be yourself'. Heart racing, I checked every letter of the alphabet to discover if any other mysterious messages would appear, somehow knowing that they would and I trembled with what I discovered:

- always be you
- always be yourself
- always on my mind
- for ever in my heart
- i love you
- love you
- never forget you
- never trust anybody but yourself
- only trust yourself
- what goes around comes around
- you are beautiful
- you are perfect

I decided to ask my iTunes [see below] who this messenger was (I regularly turn to this for answers) and out of 3248

songs, the answer given was 'soul mate'. Naturally, my mind
is blown and seeking answers. I actually believe, especially
because of the Spanish (as I know I lived before in Spain) that
I met my soul mate in a past life.

Eleanor's story demonstrates that not only is it possible to use the
internet to get messages, but also iTunes! How can this be? Well
it's just the same as using tarot cards, for instance; it's just a tool
with which we can subconsciously select a card – or a song in
Eleanor's case – to give us an answer. When you want to use this
principle, you simply ask a question of the universe (or your
higher self, if you want to call it that) and then press a random
electronic button on your iPad, stick a pin in a list of names, select
a tarot card or let a book fall open at a random page, and believe
that the answer you get, be it in the form of a word, phrase, picture, tune or whatever, is the answer you were seeking. It doesn't
matter which tool you use. It could be an angel card, dowsing
with a pendulum, choosing a song arbitrarily on a jukebox, looking at car number plates and selecting one at random or any
number of other things. All of them follow the same principle.

I have no doubt whatsoever that the methods in this chapter
work, and by trying one you have nothing to lose and, quite possibly, everything to gain. Science is catching up with ancient
mysticism. I recently watched a TV show featuring Dr Brian Cox,
the eminent physicist, who said that everything is connected to
everything else, and that the energy of each molecule has a
knock-on effect on every other one. So given the interconnected-
ness of everything, what might appear to be the random selection
of cards (or anything else) could, in fact, supply the true answer
we're seeking.

CHAPTER 9

Celebrate Finding Your Eternal Flame

Once you've found that perfect love, it's a good idea to create a special ceremony all of your own either instead of or as a complement to the traditional and legal ones. If you want to go down the traditional route of marriage, there are still ways to make it different and special. It needn't cost a fortune, and the fact that you have to put some thought and imagination into it, adds to the sense of occasion.

Put a ring on it

Think about having your wedding or commitment rings custom made. It doesn't cost as much as you think, although if you have an intricate design, you'll need to choose a hard metal such as platinum, as gold is softer and the pattern will wear away quite quickly. Silver rings are very popular nowadays too for the same reason, and are a lot less expensive.

Consider whether you want stones – and if you do, they don't have to be diamonds. If you have an old family ring – perhaps one that belonged to your great-grandmother – you might decide to use the stones from that; although the metal may have worn, the stones, especially from an older ring, will most likely have been very good quality.

Different stones have different meanings, so you can choose a stone (or a combination of stones) to give your rings a special meaning. Here are just some of the more unusual ones.

ALEXANDRITE

If you have expensive taste and a very deep pocket, the most spectacular ring stone in the world is the alexandrite. It's named after the Russian royal family who treasured it above all others. This stone can actually put a diamond to shame in the sparkle stakes, but a genuine one will cost at least £5000.

Alexandrite is said to increase confidence and self-esteem.

SPESSARTINE (ORANGE GARNET)

These come in various grades, from a rather dull one that looks a little like amber, to a perfectly clear, sparkling one, with a rich, deep colour. Your choice will depend on your budget. It's main component, and what gives it the orange colour is manganese, but the iron content will make for a much darker stone. They come in three shades: the lightest and medium colours come from Nigeria and the brightest, known as a mandarin, come from Namibia.

Spessartine is said to give strength of heart and offer protection.

WHITE TOPAZ

If cut skilfully, this can be a good alternative to diamonds, as it is quite a hard and sparkly stone. Topaz was used extensively in amulets in medieval times. It does come in a great variety of other colours too, but the clearest white ones come from Brazil. The ones that are clear are that way simply because they contain no other minerals.

White topaz is said to prevent nightmares and encourage fidelity in the wearer.

RUBELLITE (PINK TOURMALINE)

The cost of rubellite is determined by the intensity of its pink colour: the deeper the pink, the more expensive it will be. But a really crystal clear one is fairly rare. Rubellite is found mostly found in Brazil, Mozambique, Nigeria, Madagascar and Pakistan. There is also a rubellite mine in the USA.

Rubellite is said to give emotional balance and aid great communication.

KUNZITE

Kunzite is a rare and unusual gemstone ranging from almost clear to a sumptuous, electric pink. It's found in California, Brazil and Afghanistan. This is one of the few stones that cannot be synthesised, so you can be sure your stone will be a genuine one.

Kunzite is the ultimate stone for 'love'. It strengthens love of self and love of another. It is also said to heal quarrels and aid meaningful discussion.

Say it with words

It's a lovely idea to use a poem or some song lyrics to seal your union. Rather than say the words yourself though, it may be better if a third party says them on behalf of both you. Here is a good example:

> Love one another
> But make not a bond of love:
> Let it rather be a moving sea
> Between the shores of your souls.
> Fill each other's cup
> But drink not from one cup
> Give one another of your bread,
> But eat not from the same loaf.
> Sing and dance together and be joyous,
> But let each one of you be alone
> Even as the strings of the lute are alone
> Though they quiver with the same music.
> Give your hearts
> But not into each other's keeping.
> For only the hand of Life
> Can contain your hearts.
> And stand together
> Yet not too near together:
> For the pillars of the temple stand apart
> And the oak tree and the cypress
> Grow not in each other's shadow.
>
> *From* The Prophet, *Khalil Gibran*

The choices are endless and can be anything from traditional to modern, from classical to rap – whatever speaks to your heart and soul. Here are some suggestions for poems and songs that you can look up:

- 'Love Is', Adrian Henri
- 'The Confirmation', Edwin Muir
- 'Roads Go Ever On', J. R. R. Tolkien
- 'Thank You', Led Zeppelin
- 'The Luckiest', Ben Folds
- 'Be Mine', David Gray

Say it with flowers

Choose your flowers with a lot of care – not just to go with your colour scheme. Flowers really do have a language all of their own. Most people know that roses are traditionally linked with romance but here are some of the less well-known associations:

- **Larkspur**: laughter and lightness of spirit
- **Zinnia (deep red)**: lifelong devotion
- **Freesia**: absolute trust
- **Poppy**: pleasure and enduring imagination
- **Lily of the valley**: completeness
- **Hibiscus:** delicate beauty
- **Apple blossom**: admiration of wisdom and beauty
- **Aster:** patience and thoughtfulness
- **Gardenia**: secret love
- **Gloxinia**: love at first sight
- **Orchid**: fertility

Of course, you can mix any of the above together to create a more meaningful and unique message.

And, because you wouldn't want your flowers to embody the wrong message, beware of:

- **Daffodil**: unrequited love
- **Oleander**: warning
- **Antirrhinums**: deception
- **Sweet peas**: goodbye
- **Cyclamens**: resignation
- **Striped carnation**: a refusal

The right place

This is going to be a day you'll want to remember, so the place has to have the right energy for both of you. There are literally thousands of unusual places to get married and even more if you're looking for a simple blessing rather than a legal ceremony. Here are some of my favourites.

AT THE OCEAN

I love this option because I'm always happiest when in sight of the sea. Through www.devonbeachweddings.co.uk you have the choice of a thatched gazebo right on the beach, or you can have a ceremony inside the tunnels themselves. Or, if you want a cosier atmosphere, you can use the function room with a balcony over-looking the sea. This venue is licensed for civil ceremonies and civil partnerships.

AT THE ZOO

Because I love animals, this option would suit me very well. (On my thirtieth birthday Tony arranged a surprise for me so that I could feed all the big cats at Colchester Zoo in Essex – a childhood dream.) Historic Oakfield Manor, in the grounds of Chester Zoo, is licensed for weddings, civil partnerships, renewal of vows or naming ceremonies (visit www.chesterzoo.org). Of course, as well as the extensive gardens, they also have thousands of animals to give your ceremony an exotic feel.

ON A BOAT

Through www.lakemeadcruises.com, you can arrange to have your ceremony on a romantic boat right in the shadows of the famous Hoover Dam. I love the spaciousness of the USA in general and this lake is spectacular. You'll be aboard the *Desert Princess*, with up to 200 guests. The prices range widely from self-catering to champagne level.

IN A TREEHOUSE

I love trees and always wanted a treehouse as a child, but never had one. Just the name TreeHouse Point (visit www.treehousepoint. com) makes me love this venue. Set in a forest near Washington, it is the ultimate in treehouses for adults and guarantees a spectacular outlook.

IN THE RAINFOREST

Tropical sounds and thick green rainforest make a lovely picture in my head for a great place to exchange vows. The Bundaleer Rainforest Gardens (http://bundaleer.com) are situated just 18 kilometres from Brisbane, but you'll think you're in the middle of an untamed jungle. There is a choice of venues, including the 'baby waterfall' and the 'Treetops Room' – see www.myweddinghour.com.au.

IN THE MOUNTAINS

Spicers Peak Lodge in Australia (http://spicersgroup.com.au) is set on the crest of a mountain and offers expansive views of the surrounding National Parks and the Great Dividing Range. This is somewhere you can really feel 'on top of the world'!

Of course, if you'd rather not – or can't afford – to spend a lot of time and money either travelling yourself or transporting relatives to somewhere exotic, why not look into using your local woodland or forest and create a bower of flowers to rival the splendour of unusual locations with simple, yet breathtaking beauty?

The right time

There are several ways you can go about choosing the most auspicious date to be married or commit to a lifelong partnership.

NUMEROLOGY

One way I like for choosing a date is using numerology. We all have a life-path number, which we can find out by using our date of birth. For instance, if your birthday is on 21 June 1981, then your life-path number will be $2 + 1 + 0 + 6 + 1 + 9 + 8 + 1$, which equals 28. You then reduce this figure down to a single digit, first by adding 2 and 8 together which equals 10, then by adding $1 + 0$ to get to 1. So if your partner's date of birth is 16 May 1975, their life-path number will be $1 + 6 + 0 + 5 + 1 + 9 + 7 + 5$, which = 34, and $3 + 4 = 7$. Add your own and your partner's life-path dates together to get your joint life-path or marriage/union number. (Remember, if you end up with a double digit, add the two digits together to make a single-digit number.)

Once you have your number, all you have to do is calculate a date that adds up to the same number in the year you're getting married/forming a civil partnership. So for instance, if you add up together to a number 3, then your preferred wedding date would be one that reduces to a 3. For instance: 2 March 2014, would be $0 + 2 + 0 + 3 + 2 + 0 + 1 + 4 = 12$, and $1 + 2 = 3$.

IT'S IN THE STARS

Astrology is a time-honoured way to choose a lucky day that's been used since Roman times and beyond. Certain times, such as those of the planets' retrograde (which is when their orbits appear to slow down or even go backwards) are thought to bring a bit of chaos to our lives, so wedding plans can tend to go awry on these dates. Eclipses can also be problematic. In order to avoid these, visit www.skyscript.co.uk/eclipse to find out when they fall.

On the other hand, dates to be aware of in the context of specific star signs are as follows:

ARIES

- **18 August:** a good time for romance, so if the wedding is going to be traditional hearts and flowers, this would be a good date

- **23 August:** for a more practical couple who have carefully weighed up all the pros and cons, this date is an auspicious choice

- **27 August:** a couple who feel they need the help and guidance of a mother or another close family female, will find this date brings them the feeling of security they seek

TAURUS

- **6 February:** this is a 'for ever' date, so if the couple want to be sure that love lasts, this would be a very good day to make extra sure that the fascination endures

- **30 July:** for a relationship that is all about creating a family, this is the date that will ensure fertility and abundance

- **18 September:** this should be called Eternal Flame day because on this date, as they gaze into each other's eyes, the couple may well recall past lives they spent together

GEMINI

- **5 February:** there are exciting times ahead for the couple who choose this date; their passion will lead them to unexpected places and every day will be an adventure

- **8 October:** this is the date for the couple who long for an end to old conflicts and a new beginning on an equal playing field; there will be a balance for them of play and work

- **17 October:** this is a passionate day which could bring arguments during the wedding, but with clear discussion beforehand, all will be well

CANCER

- **6 February:** another date for prospective parents as it will also bring great fertility; this couple will never lose their childhood joy and will make great – if very lenient – parents

- **18 September:** this date will suit the couple who love children and will enjoy having at least ten bridesmaids and pageboys, if funds allow; their menu should include tea favourites, such as jelly and blancmange to ensure a party mood

- **23 December:** this wedding might appear to have disaster potential, but it's not so; the couple will laugh and joke all the way through, demonstrating their promise for a good marriage

LEO

- **5 February:** if one person has planned a surprise honeymoon, this is the date when the surprise will work best and the couple who choose it will always be romantic
- **8 February:** this date will be one huge party for two 'party animals'; they'll need a large venue with a big entertaining area and plenty of cash to enjoy their social whirl of a wedding
- **15 April:** this date is for the couple who are seriously into home-making; it will be a modest wedding, otherwise they may later regret the cash wasted on 'bling'

VIRGO

- **26 October:** this is the ultimate date for the couple who are party animals; they will live fast and loose and enjoy flirting with friends
- **16 November:** tantric sex is the order of the day for this couple; mystical and aware, they'll probably go for a venue in the middle of a jungle or forest, perhaps with a 'hippy' theme
- **23 December:** this is the date for a couple who will adore and live for their children, always willing to work hard to give them the best possible home and future

LIBRA

- **8 February:** this date is for a couple who should have been around in the 1960s, when they would have been free lovers; they will love nature and enjoy an open-air ceremony (weather permitting) or, if not, a venue decorated with fresh greenery

- **15 February:** a union on this date will rekindle passion, and will be a very suitable day for an older couple who have perhaps been married before, or have been together for a long time before making any vows

- **15 April:** this will be the couple that others envy because the strength of their commitment to each other will be so obvious in their personalised vows on this date; it's hard to see anything going wrong with their day

SCORPIO

- **20 April:** a good date for the couple who have been hurt in the past and are relying on each other to heal their wounds and scars from previous relationships

- **24 April:** this is the date for the lucky couple who win the lottery or are always winning competitions; they will make good decisions and good bets both in their relationship and in business

- **20 July:** this date is for couples who opt for a private affair, as they are likely to sit up all night talking; they will never run out of conversation because they'll find each other endlessly fascinating

SAGITTARIUS

- **15 February:** on this date the sky's the limit with regard to venues and budgets because this couple will seem to have the Midas touch – everything they try appears to work

- **2 April:** this is one of the best dates in the year to get married; the energy around the couple and their ceremony will be calm and beautiful, whatever the weather, as will be their journey through life together

- **10 May:** this is the date for the couple who do love each other, but aren't going to be clingy; they'll give each other space and allow each other to breathe

CAPRICORN

- **24 April:** on this date the bride and groom will glow with inner beauty and be unafraid to wear the most outrageous clothes; no one will take their eyes off them

- **27 September:** on this date the couple will receive the most incredible and expensive wedding gifts, so it's worthwhile for them to put together a great gift list

- **21 October:** this date will be quite manic, and so will the couple's lives, but that will suit them as they are easily bored when things are too quiet

AQUARIUS

- **15 February:** this is a date when parents might be tempted to embarrass the bride and groom with tales of past exploits, but this couple have the ability to laugh at themselves, and this will only bring them closer together

- **2 April:** this date is for a sexy couple who will wear unconventional clothes and have their ceremony in a most unusual place; their partnership will continue to be 'off the wall'

- **8 July:** there may be an argument on or near this date, but after the ceremony the couple will find new understanding and a blissful partnership will be formed

PISCES

- **30 July:** this date will be a good one to sort out family feuds and heal rifts; it will also be a good date for the business-minded couple to do some networking

- **21 October:** a date to remember in every sense; this couple will never forget an anniversary or birthday

- **7 November:** an exciting and surprising day; this couple will learn a great deal about each other, but it will all be good

Of course, you may well each have a different star sign, so you'll need to select the best day out of all the possible choices for each of you. Use as many of the auspicious numbers in combination as you can. For instance, if one of you is a Pisces and the other a

Capricorn, you could choose from either sign's good dates, i.e. 30, 7 and 21, and 24, 27 and 21. Any numbers you share – in this case 21 – would be very good ones to start with. You can use all these numbers if you're clever, for time of day as well as actual date. Obviously, if the exact same date appears on both your charts, then that is the day to go for.

It's important to read the meanings too, of course, and if one explanation resonates most strongly with what you both want from a marriage, then go for that. In a conventional horoscope, you have to take into account the day, time of day and place you were born, as well as the star sign, to avoid mistakes. However, by injecting your strong intent and the science of numerology into the equation you really can get it right in the ways I have suggested.

Conclusion

Whether you're happily partnered or you're still looking, I hope you've learned a lot about yourself and your relationships from this book. Whether you've decided to delve into past lives with your existing partner to see if there is another dimension to your relationship or you've decided to seek clues to your soul mate's whereabouts and history with you through your past lives, I can assure you the search will be fulfilling and very much worthwhile.

If someone has broken your heart, I hope you can take solace from the knowledge that he or she was not actually your Eternal Flame, and that by leaving you they have made way for that soul mate to come into your life.

If your soul mate has passed over, it should be of some comfort to know that because the biggest parts of each of you remain with their presence in heaven, you will never, in fact, be parted – even if one of you is stuck on the earth plane for some time.

And remember that before coming to this lifetime as reincarnated souls we all understood exactly what needed to happen here and agreed to do it, if we possibly could, so as long as you follow the signs and your rightful path, doing what you always believe to be right and honourable, then your soul mate will find you, in whatever form they take in this life, and they will help you.

Appendix

Here's just a small selection of the many lovely anecdotal accounts that people have sent me describing how they feel about their soul mates.

Liz

I knew the minute I met him, and still feel the same forty years on.

Jenny

I've always felt my late husband Alan was my soul mate because even though he passed over three years ago, I still feel him around me. Though he isn't here physically, I still feel deeply connected to him spiritually.

Lynn

My husband Roger is my soul mate. There was such a deep connection between us as soon as we met, like we'd met before somewhere, and it was – and still is – easy to be with him. There are no dramas, just a lovely, easy relationship.

We've been together for thirteen years and he's there to ground me and support me in the work I do.

Nina

It's his eyes. When I see them I feel like I know them, like I know the person inside. My world feels like it revolves around this person, and I can't forget him, no matter what. It's a deep feeling: you see this person and something inside you moves, emotionally. I believe that if/when you meet, no matter how shy or self-conscious you are, it will all just melt away at that moment, as you feel so at ease with one another.

Amanda

I've met my soul mate. It was his whole energy. I felt totally at one with him, even though he is seven years younger than me. Every sense and every cell in my body stood on end. It was like a shiver down your spine when something resonates deep within your very essence.

Erica

I met my soul mate and was instantly drawn to him. When we look at each other there's a connection, an unspoken communication of souls. He's often told me that I see right into his soul when I look at him. In fact, we're divorced now, and so I've learned that even if you are soul mates, you don't always remain together or even become a couple at all. It's difficult to let go of your soul mate (almost feels like you have lost a piece of yourself). Will I meet another soul mate in this lifetime, I wonder? I haven't as yet, but I'll know him as soon as we look at each other.

♡♡Kerry

We've had our troubles, but Matt's been my rock and is always there for me just when I need him. We're right for each other and love each other very much, and I'd be nowhere without him – literally. We spend all of our time together and we just gel. I owe him my life and give him my unconditional love.

♡♡Karen

I met my soul mate when I was twelve; our eyes met and that was that. He's the only one I've ever felt this strongly about. He doesn't just make me smile on the outside; he makes my heart and soul smile too. I now know the feelings I have for him are because we are Twin soul mates. Unfortunately though, we're not meant to be together in life. He died when I was nineteen, but within hours he was by my side as a spirit, explaining our connection. He has remained by my side as my main guide ever since – almost thirty-one years now!

♡♡Carmen

I saw my soul mate in a drive-through. He was in a car going the opposite way. It felt like time didn't exist; nothing around me existed. I couldn't talk, couldn't move a muscle. Our eyes

met and that was 'it'. I wanted to run to his car and shout,
'Where have you been? I've been waiting for you, why did
you leave me alone?' Although that was the only time I've
ever seen him in this lifetime, I know he is my soul mate. I
know that one day, albeit on the 'other side', we'll be
together again. He is the love of my life for eternity.

Linda

I was seventeen and was asked to go on a blind date with
my sister. I agreed because without ever having seen him I
knew that this man would be my soul mate and that I would
spend my life with him. We met on 1 December 1973 and
were married the next May. Everybody said it wouldn't last,
but we're still as happy and in love as we were way back
then, and have four grown-up children. We each know what
the other's thinking and often say the same thing at the same
time. We know we'll be together for ever and have shared
many lives and could never imagine being apart.

Rachel

My partner told me that he asked the universe for me, and
I came. It took me years to get out of him what exactly he
asked for.

Anne

I'm happily married to my soul mate of twenty-plus years. As
soon as we met I heard the word 'home'.

There was definitely 'someone' working overtime to get

us together. I hadn't planned on being where I was. He had planned on being there with someone else. As we talked, he answered questions on many subjects just before I was about to ask them, and he still does that. If there's such a thing as a Twin soul or soul mate, I found mine.

Rosey

It's right to say that my hubby is my soul mate because I wouldn't be who I am without him. He's the other half of my heart, my rock of strength when I feel down, and it took moving 900 miles to find him. I'd do it again in a heartbeat because I've found my best friend.

Resources

For hypnotherapy, I strongly recommend Jacqueline Kirtley (www.oasishypnotherapy.co.uk). I have used Jacqueline myself and a more caring, compassionate and skilled practitioner would be hard to find. However, on my website (www.jenny smedley.com) you can also find a list of other suitable therapists worldwide.

To find out more about how love can perform miracles, visit www.alyssaphillipsinc.com. Alyssa and her husband Neil live in Atlanta, Georgia and are happier, healthier and more in love than ever before. You can read more about their story, see photos, updates and more on Alyssa's website. Alyssa now reaches out to help others by sharing her story and the miracle of love, hope and faith and is currently writing her first book.

To connect with women around the world, visit www.nancyal varezwrites.com. Nancy specialises in writing for women. She has been on an incredible journey of empowerment and helps women to become independently happy.

For angel help, visit www.jackynewcomb.com. Jacky Newcomb, known as the 'Angel Lady' has been a great mentor and help to me personally. She and her husband John are a match made in heaven.

For help with your soul-mate journey, visit Barbara Meiklejohn-Free's website at www.spiritvisions.co.uk/index.htm. Barbara is a wonderful example of how to follow the signs to your soul mates, and can certainly give you the benefit of her experiences to help you follow yours.

For more advice on animal soul mates, visit Madeleine Walker's website at www.anexchangeoflove.com. Madeleine conducts workshops all over the world and has been featured in countless radio shows. She visits animals in their homes to communicate with them and also does telephone and email consultations.

Also visit Jackie Weaver's website at www.animal psychic.co.uk. Jackie's personal story of total recovery from an apparently fatal illness is an amazing one. She has since communicated with many celebrities' pets.

To watch or read about strange animal soul mates, check out http://natgeotv.com/uk/bizarre-animal-friends/galleries/odd-couples, www.care2.com/greenliving/9-amazing-animal-friendship. html and http://webecoist.momtastic.com/2010/03 /25/bizarre-bffs-unlikely-but-awwwsome-animal-friends-pics/.

For help if you feel you need to travel to find your soul mate, visit www.wesaidgotravel.com. Lisa and George Rajna spent eleven months wandering across Southeast Asia from Indonesia to Mongolia, where they fell in love, got engaged and now, as a married couple, are writing a book together about their journey.

For a psychic look at soul mates, visit Maggie Sinton's website on www.gypsymaggierose.com. For readers in Australia, Maggie is available in person to give you help on the psychic side. She also does seminars and workshops, as well as email consultations.

To find a penpal in prison, contact PrisonPenPals, PO Box 235, East Berlin, PA, 17316-0235, USA.

To find a British penpal, write to British Penpals, 36, The King's Gap, Hoylake, Wirral, CH47 1HF.

To find a surrogate family, visit Big Brothers and Big Sisters at www.bbbs.org or for surrogate grandparents, www.grandparents.com.

Recommended Reading

Barbara Meiklejohn-Free, *The Heart of All Knowing: Awakening your inner self*, O Books, 2007

Jacky Newcomb, *Healed By An Angel: True stories of healing miracles*, Hay House, 2011

Madeleine Walker, *Your Pets' Past Lives & How They Can Heal You*, Findhorn Press, 2012

Jackie Weaver, *Celebrity Pet Talking*, Upfront Publishing, 2011

About the Author

Based in beautiful Somerset, in the UK, and happily married for over forty-two years, Jenny Smedley DPLT is a qualified past-life regressionist, an author, TV and radio presenter, international columnist and spiritual consultant, specialising in the subjects of past lives and angels.

Her own life was turned around by a vision from her one of her past lives, in which she had met the man known today as Garth Brooks (see pp. 48–55), and as a result of which problems and issues related to that life were healed and resolved in a few seconds. For two years she hosted her own spiritual chat show on Taunton TV, interviewing people such as David Icke, Reg Presley, Uri Geller and Diana Cooper. Jenny has appeared on many TV shows in the UK, USA, Ireland and Australia, including, *The Big Breakfast*, *Kelly*, *Open House*, *The Heaven and Earth Show*, *Kilroy* and *Jane Goldman Investigates*, as well as hundreds of radio shows, including *The Steve Wright Show* on Radio 2 and *The Richard Bacon Show* on '5 live' in the UK, and others in the USA, Australia, New Zealand, Iceland, Tasmania, the Caribbean, South Africa and Spain.

Jenny has recently been featured in the *Daily Mail*, *Daily Express* and the *Sunday Times Style* magazine. Jenny's website is:

www.jennysmedley.com. She'd love to hear from you about your soul mate, so please get in touch by emailing her on: author@global net.co.uk and perhaps you will be immortalised in another of her books.

Index

Also from Piatkus:

CALL ME WHEN YOU GET TO HEAVEN

Our amazing true story of messages from the other side

Jacky Newcomb and Madeline Richardson

In this fascinating and moving memoir, renowned 'angel lady' Jacky Newcomb and her sister Madeline share the communications they have received from their beloved father, Ron, since he passed away in 2008. Ron reaches out to them from 'the other side' to show his family that there most certainly is life after death.

Ron visits his family and friends in dreams and shows them the future in visions. He reaches out to them to prove that he is safe in the afterlife, and to offer reassurance and guidance from the world beyond.

This extraordinary book shows that this life is not the end, and that happiness can be found in the afterlife. It is a touching and emotional tribute by two daughters to their father that will offer comfort and hope to anyone who has lost someone they love.

978-0-7499-5661-5

THE SPIRIT OF LOVE

Two psychics and their messages from the other side

Paul Norton and Tracy Hall

Paul Norton and Tracy Hall are an ordinary couple with
an extraordinary story to tell.

Disillusioned that her spirit friends had not warned her that her brother was
about to commit suicide, grieving medium Tracy Hall decided that she no
longer wanted to use her own gifts to help others. Some months later,
she went with her mother to see well-known psychic Paul Norton at a
spiritualist meeting. There, he gave her a message which would change
her life. Through Paul, Tracy's brother told her not to give up her work
and that help was on its way.

Soon after, Paul invited Tracy to work with him. Together they embarked on
a journey of spiritual discovery that also led to a blossoming relationship.
They are now dedicated to each other and to sharing messages from the
other side with the many people who come to see them. The Spirit of Love
shares the moving story of how fate brought them together, and is packed
with amazing and uplifting stories about the work they do.

978-0-7499-2848-3

WORKING WITH SPIRIT GUIDES

How to meet, communicate with and be protected by your guide

Ruth White

Do we all have guides? If so, who are they and what do they do? In *Working with Spirit Guides*, Ruth White explains all you need to know about these special beings: what their purpose is in our lives, how to identify and communicate with them and what to expect from them.

The easy-to-follow exercises will show you how to work with your dreams and intuition, guard against false guidance, ask you spirit guides the right questions and learn how to recognise the right answers, so that you can discover your sense of purpose and follow your destiny.

978-0-7499-4045-4

ANGEL MAGIC

Angel inspiration for busy people

Cassandra Eason

In the frantic modern world we all want to discover easy way to improve the harmony of our lives, reduce stress and resolve problems.

Whether you're an angel expert or simply want to incorporate some spirituality into a busy lifestyle, *Angel Magic* will show you how to recognise the angels that are all around you to improve every aspect of your life.

Filled with inspirational anecdotes and practical exercises, and including a directory of 250 angels for you to call on, Angel Magic shows you how to harness the ancient power of angels to enrich your life quickly and easily.

978-0-7499-4096-6

JOURNEYS THROUGH TIME

Uncovering my past lives

Jenny Cockell

Jenny Cockell has always had memories of living before. In her first groundbreaking book, Yesterday's Children, she described her search for the past-life family that had haunted her from earliest childhood. She remembered living as Mary Sutton, an Irishwoman who had died more than twenty years before she was born. She gave an extraordinary account of how she successfully found Mary's surviving children, and was reunited with them in the present.

Journeys Through Time continues her quest to discover her past lives. Jenny gives details of the four past lives that she remembers most clearly and explains how she has tried to trace them all. It is a page-turning account of one woman's journey to find the lives she lived before and how this, in turn, has helped her to understand and enhance her life now.

978-0-7499-2944-2